Tower Vortx Digital Air Fryer Oven

Cookbook UK 2023

Quick & Delicious Tower Air Fryer Recipes For Beginners & Advance Users

Bethany Nicholls

Contents

INTRODUCTION 5

BREAKFAST RECIPES 8

Healthy Breakfast Cookies 9

Easy Egg Quiche...10

Fluffy Frittata With Bell Pepper.......................10

Air Fried Cream Cheese Wontons...................11

Meat Lover Omelet With Mozzarella 12

Creamy Potato Gratin With Nutmeg................12

Salty Parsnip Patties 13

Glazed Strawberry Toast 13

Olive & Tomato Tart With Feta Cheese 14

Cabbage And Pork Gyoza................................15

Cinnamon French Toasts.................................16

Smart Oven Baked Oatmeal Recipe 17

LUNCH RECIPES 18

Zucchini And Cauliflower Stew 19

Chicken Potato Bake.......................................19

Sweet & Sour Pork 20

Beef Steaks With Beans 21

Fried Chicken Tacos 22

Squash And Zucchini Mini Pizza 23

Spicy Avocado Cauliflower Toast.....................24

Country Comfort Corn Bread...........................25

Air Fried Sausages 25

Cheese-stuffed Meatballs 26

Ground Chicken Meatballs 27

DINNER RECIPES..28

Zingy Dilled Salmon...29

Greek-style Monkfish With Vegetables............30

Filet Mignon With Chili Peanut Sauce 31

Miso-glazed Salmon 32

Lamb Skewers 32

Shrimp Scampi 33

Buttered Scallops 33

Bacon Pork Bites 34

Basil Tomatoes 35

Italian Shrimp Scampi......................................35

Crumbly Oat Meatloaf......................................36

SNACKS AND DESSERTS RECIPES 37

Lemon Bars 38

Quick Coffee Cake 38

Chocolate Ramekins 39

Coconut Cookies With Pecans 40

Roasted Chickpeas 41

Coffee Chocolate Cake 42

Vanilla Rum Cookies With Walnuts 43

Easy Air Fryer Tofu 44

Apricot Crumble With Blackberries..................44

Ultimate Coconut Chocolate Cake 45

Honey And Orange Pancakes 46

MEAT RECIPES 47

Baked Beef & Broccoli.....................................48

Savory Buffalo Chicken 48

Air Fry Chicken Drumsticks 49

Herb Pork Tenderloin...................................49

Pork Sausage With Cauliflower Mash 50

Chicken Parm 51

opycat Taco Bell Crunch Wraps 52

Salsa Beef Meatballs................................53

Cheese Chicken Fries 54

Air Fryer Juicy Pork Chops.....................55

Pork Sticks With Red Chili Flakes 56

FISH & SEAFOOD RECIPES 57

Crispy Paprika Fish Fillets (2).........................58

Old Bay Tilapia Fillets..................................58

Crab Cakes..59

Panko Catfish Nuggets................................60

Fish Spicy Lemon Kebab...............................61

Crispy Salmon With Lemon-butter Sauce 62

Cajun Red Snapper 63

Parmesan Fish Fillets 64

Baked Spinach Tilapia 65

Lobster Tails With Lemon-garlic Sauce 65

aked Spinach Tilapia 66

Saucy Cod With Green Onions 66

MEATLESS RECIPES 67

Paprika Cauliflower...68

Roasted Butternut Squash With Maple Syrup..68

Cauliflower Gnocchi's 69

Rosemary Roasted Squash With Cheese........70

Black Gram French Cuisine Galette 71

Chili Cottage Cheese...................................72

Mushroom Marinade Cutlet 73

Carrot & Chickpea Oat Balls With Cashews.....74

Potato Club Barbeque Sandwich..................75

Parmesan Breaded Zucchini Chips 76

Cottage Cheese Fingers..............................77

APPETIZERS AND SIDE DISHES 78

Mashed Turnips 79

Herbed Radish Sauté (2)...............................79

Honey Corn Muffins 80

Cheesy Broccoli Gratin.................................81

Roasted Beets With Grapefruit Glaze 82

Cheddar Tortilla Chips 83

Air Fried Eggplant Cubes 83

Herb Balsamic Mushrooms 84

Spicy Brussels Sprouts (2) 84

Buttered Corn 85

Rosemary Roasted Potatoes.........................86

OTHER FAVORITE RECIPES 87

Lush Seafood Casserole 88

Parsnip Fries With Garlic-yogurt Dip 89

Southwest Corn And Bell Pepper Roast...........90

Roasted Mushrooms 91

Classic Worcestershire Poutine......................92

Arancini...93

Chicken Sausage And Broccoli Casserole 94

Classic Churros 95

Chicken Ham Casserole.............................96

Sumptuous Beef And Bean Chili Casserole 97

Simple Cheesy Shrimps 98

INTRODUCTION

An air fryer oven is a full-sized oven that features an air fry cooking mode integrated within the oven cavity. With this innovative technology, you can now enjoy all of the benefits of air fry no matter what kind of range you're looking for - induction, gas, or electric. By using a high-powered fan to circulate hot air around the food at a high speed, our in-range air fry feature cooks ingredients to a perfectly crisped finish.

The Benefits of an Air Frying Oven

An air frying oven uses little to no oil to create a flavorful and crunchy texture on foods and boasts all of the same benefits as a standalone air fryer - with some additional conveniences.

1. The air fry feature is integrated right into your oven, eliminating the need to store an extra appliance or take up valuable counter space.

2. An air frying oven has more capacity, saving you time and allowing you to cook more food at once so that there's always enough for the whole family.

3. A Frigidaire Air Fry Oven does more than just air fry, so one appliance works harder for you. Enjoy other features such as Even Baking with True Convection, Fast Steam Cleaning, and Smudge-Proof® Stainless Steel.

What Foods Can You Cook in an Air Frying Oven?

An air fryer oven does a delicious job at cooking most traditional deep-fried foods and these are some of our favorites:

- Sweet Potato or French fries
- Chicken wings or tenders
- Zucchini fries
- Onion rings
- Pepperoni pizza rolls
- Mac 'n' cheese
- Brussel sprouts

How do I keep my air frying oven clean?

Before using the air fry feature, place a cookie or baking sheet a rack or two under the Air Fry Tray to catch crumbs or drips. This will keep the bottom of the oven clean and free of fallen bits that can burn or cause odors later. Remember, do not place pans directly on the oven bottom to keep heat circulating correctly.

How do I clean the Air Fry Tray?

The Air Fry Tray is dishwasher safe, but for optimal cleaning, we recommend washing it by hand. It's designed to hold foods that already have some oil on them, which should keep food from sticking.

How do I limit the amount of smoke when using the Air Fry Tray?

Air fry uses really hot air to cook food fast and make it crunchy. Although air fry uses hot air to cook, remember that you are still frying your food so that it gets crispy! When some high-fat or greasy foods (like fresh wings) meet that hot air inside an oven, some smoke is normal. **If air fry is making a lot of smoke, try these tips:**

- When using the Air Fry Tray, put a baking sheet on a rack or two below the Air Fry Tray. This keeps drips and crumbs from landing on the oven bottom, where they can burn and create smoke. For additional protection, place some foil-lined parchment paper on the baking sheet. Parchment paper traps oil and keeps it from smoking.

- Use cooking oils that can stand up to high temperatures like avocado, grapeseed, and peanut oils. Cooking sprays made from these oils are available at the grocery store.

- Keep foil, parchment paper, and bakeware off the bottom of the oven. The oven bottom needs to stay clear so air can circulate.

- Don't overcrowd the food on your baking sheet or on the Air Fry Tray. If air can't circulate around each item, the cooking and crisping process may slow down and allow more grease to settle or drip.

- If your catch-tray is smoking, try placing parchment paper on it to hold grease. For extra-moist foods, you may have to use more. It's worth it!

- Some foods, like fresh wings and some vegetables, have a lot of moisture and may drip more than you expect. For items that might drip, use a pan with low sides if you're not using an Air Fry Tray.

- Air fry uses super-heated air, so if your oven bottom already has drips or crumbs on it (it happens!), those can smoke. Keep your oven bottom clean.

- If you have an oven vent, use it when cooking with air fry, like you would when using the cooktop.

BREAKFAST RECIPES

Healthy Breakfast Cookies

Ingredients:

Servings: 12
Cooking Time:
15 Mins.

» 2 C. quick oats

» 1/4 C. chocolate chips

» 1 1/2 tbsp. chia seeds

» 1/4 C. shredded coconut

» 1/2 C. mashed banana

» 1/4 C. applesauce

» 1/4 C. honey

» 1/2 tsp cinnamon

» 3/4 C. almond butter

Directions:

1. Fit the Cuisinart oven with the rack in position

2. Line baking pan with parchment paper and set aside.

3. Add all ingredients into the mixing bowl and mix until well combined.

4. Using a cookie scoop drop 12 scoops of oat mixture onto a prepared baking pan and lightly flatten the cookie.

5. Set to bake at 325 F for 20 minutes. After 5 minutes place the baking pan in the preheated oven.

6. Serve and enjoy.

Easy Egg Quiche

Ingredients:

» 8 eggs

» 4 tbsp. butter, melted

» 6 oz cream cheese

» 6 oz cheddar cheese, shredded

Servings: 6
Cooking Time:
45 Mins.

Directions:

1. Fit the Cuisinart oven with the rack in position

2. Add eggs, cheese, butter, and cream cheese into the bowl and whisk until well combined.

3. Pour egg mixture into the greased pie dish.

4. Set to bake at 325 F for 50 minutes, after 5 minutes, place the pie dish in the oven.

5. Serve and enjoy.

Fluffy Frittata With Bell Pepper

Ingredients:

» 8 eggs

» 2 tbsp. whole milk

» 1 tbsp. butter

» Coarse salt, freshly ground pepper, to taste

» ½ zucchini diced

» 1 bell Pepper seeded and diced

Servings: x
Cooking Time: x

Directions:

1. Preheat oven to 400°F.

2. Heat Breville smart oven over medium heat. Add butter.

3. In a bowl, add remaining ingredients. Pour mixture into Breville smart oven.

4. When eggs are half set and edges begin to pull away, place frittata in

5. the oven and bake for about 10 minutes, or until center is no longer jiggly.

6. Cut into wedges or slide out onto serving plate.

Air Fried Cream Cheese Wontons

Ingredients:

» 2 oz. (57 g) cream cheese, softened

» 1 tbsp. sugar

» 16 square wonton wrappers

» Cooking spray

Servings: 4
Cooking Time: 6 Mins.

Directions:

1. Spritz the air fryer basket with cooking spray.

2. In a mixing bowl, stir together the cream cheese and sugar until well mixed. Prepare a small bowl of water alongside.

3. On a clean work surface, lay the wonton wrappers. Scoop ¼ tsp. of cream cheese in the center of each wonton wrapper. Dab the water over the wrapper edges. Fold each wonton wrapper diagonally in half over the filling to form a triangle.

4. Arrange the wontons in the pan. Spritz the wontons with cooking spray.

5. Put the air fryer basket on the baking pan and slide into Rack Position 2, select Air Fry, set temperature to 350°F (180°C) and set time to 6 minutes.

6. Flip the wontons halfway through the cooking time.

7. When cooking is complete, the wontons will be golden brown and crispy.

8. Divide the wontons among four plates. Let rest for 5 minutes before serving.

Meat Lover Omelet With Mozzarella

Ingredients:

» 1 beef sausage, chopped

» 4 slices prosciutto, chopped

» 3 oz salami, chopped

» 1 C. grated mozzarella cheese

» 4 eggs

» 1 tbsp. chopped onion

» 1 tbsp. ketchup

Servings: 2
Cooking Time:
20 Mins.

Directions:

1. Preheat Breville on Bake function to 350 F. Whisk the eggs with ketchup in a bowl. Stir in the onion. Brown the sausage in a greased pan over medium heat for 2 minutes.

2. Combine the egg mixture, mozzarella cheese, salami, and prosciutto. Pour the egg mixture over the sausage and give it a stir. Press Start and cook in the Breville for 15 minutes.

Creamy Potato Gratin With Nutmeg

Ingredients:

» 1 lb potatoes, peeled and sliced

» ½ C. sour cream

» ½ C. mozzarella cheese, grated

» ½ C. milk

» ½ tsp nutmeg

» Salt and black pepper to taste

Servings: 4
Cooking Time:
30 Mins.

Directions:

1. Preheat Breville on Bake function to 390 F. In a bowl, combine sour cream, milk, pepper, salt, and nutmeg. Place the potato slices in the bowl with the milk mixture and stir to coat well.

2. Transfer the mixture to a baking dish and press Start. Cook for 20 minutes, then sprinkle grated cheese on top and cook for 5 more minutes. Serve warm.

Salty Parsnip Patties

Ingredients:

Servings: 2
Cooking Time:
20 Mins.

» 1 large parsnip, grated

» 3 eggs, beaten

» ½ tsp garlic powder

» ¼ tsp nutmeg

» 1 tbsp. olive oil

» 1 C. flour

» Salt and black pepper to taste

Directions:

1. In a bowl, combine flour, eggs, parsnip, nutmeg, and garlic powder. Season with salt and pepper. Form patties out of the mixture. Drizzle the AirFryer basket with olive oil and arrange the patties inside. Fit in the baking tray and cook for 15 minutes on Air Fry function at 360 F. Serve with garlic mayo.

Glazed Strawberry Toast

Ingredients:

Servings: 4
Cooking Time: 8
Mins.

» 4 slices bread, ½-inch thick

» 1 C. sliced strawberries

» 1 tsp. sugar

» Cooking spray

Directions:

1. On a clean work surface, lay the bread slices and spritz one side of each slice of bread with cooking spray.
2. Place the bread slices in the air fryer basket, sprayed side down. Top with the strawberries and a sprinkle of sugar.
3. Put the air fryer basket on the baking pan and slide into Rack Position 2, select Air Fry, set temperature to 375ºF (190ºC), and set time to 8 minutes.
4. When cooking is complete, the toast should be well browned on each side. Remove from the oven to a plate and serve.

Olive & Tomato Tart With Feta Cheese

Ingredients:

Servings: 2
Cooking Time:
25 Mins.

» 4 eggs

» ½ C. tomatoes, chopped

» 1 C. feta cheese, crumbled

» 1 tbsp. fresh basil, chopped

» 1 tbsp. fresh oregano, chopped

» ¼ C. Kalamata olives, chopped

» ¼ C. onion, chopped

» 2 tbsp. olive oil

» ½ C. milk

» Salt and black pepper to taste

Directions:

1. Preheat Cuisinart on Bake function to 360 F. Brush a pie pan with olive oil. Beat the eggs along with the milk, salt, and pepper. Stir in all of the remaining ingredients. Pour the egg mixture into the pan. Cook for 20 minutes.

Cabbage And Pork Gyoza

Ingredients:

» 1 lb. (454 g) ground pork

» 1 head Napa cabbage (about 1 lb. / 454 g), sliced thinly and minced

» ½ C. minced scallions

» 1 tsp. minced fresh chives

» 1 tsp. soy sauce

» 1 tsp. minced fresh ginger

» 1 tbsp. minced garlic

» 1 tsp. granulated sugar

» 2 tsp. kosher salt

» 48 to 50 wonton or dumpling wrappers

» Cooking spray

Directions:

1. Spritz the air fryer basket with cooking spray. Set aside.

2. Make the filling: Combine all the ingredients, except for the wrappers in a large bowl. Stir to mix well.

3. Unfold a wrapper on a clean work surface, then dab the edges with a little water. Scoop up 2 tsp. of the filling mixture in the center.

4. Make the gyoza: Fold the wrapper over to filling and press the edges to seal. Pleat the edges if desired. Repeat with remaining wrappers and fillings.

5. Arrange the gyozas in the pan and spritz with cooking spray.

6. Put the air fryer basket on the baking pan and slide into Rack Position 2, select Air Fry, set temperature to 360°F (182°C) and set time to 10 minutes.

7. Flip the gyozas halfway through the cooking time.

8. When cooked, the gyozas will be golden brown.

9. Serve immediately.

Cinnamon French Toasts

Ingredients:

Servings: 2
Cooking Time: 5 Mins.

» 2 eggs

» ¼ C. whole milk

» 3 tbsp. sugar

» 2 tsp. olive oil

» 1/8 tsp. vanilla extract

» 1/8 tsp. ground cinnamon

» 4 bread slices

Directions:

1. In a large bowl, mix together all the ingredients except bread slices.
2. Coat the bread slices with egg mixture evenly.
3. Press "Power Button" of Air Fry Oven and turn the dial to select the "Air Fry" mode.
4. Press the Time button and again turn the dial to set the cooking time to 6 minutes.
5. Now push the Temp button and rotate the dial to set the temperature at 390 degrees F.
6. Press "Start/Pause" button to start.
7. When the unit beeps to show that it is preheated, open the lid and lightly, grease the sheet pan.
8. Arrange the bread slices into "Air Fry Basket" and insert in the oven.
9. Flip the bread slices once halfway through.
10. Serve warm.

Smart Oven Baked Oatmeal Recipe

Ingredients:

Servings: x
Cooking Time: x

» 1 small Ripe Banana, (6 inches long, abut 1/4 C. mashed)

» 1 tbsp. Flax Meal

» 1/2 C. Non-Dairy Milk, plus 2 tbsp. (like Almond Milk or Soy Milk)

» 1 C. Old Fashioned Rolled Oats

» 2 tsp. Pure Maple Syrup

» 2 tsp. Olive Oil

» 1/2 tsp. Ground Cinnamon

» 1/2 tsp. Pure Vanilla Extract

» 1/4 tsp. Baking Powder

» 1/8 tsp. Fine Sea Salt

» 1/4 C. Pecan Pieces, (1 ounce)

Directions:

1. Adjust the cooking rack to the bottom position and preheat toaster oven to 350°F on the BAKE setting. Grease a 7 x 5-inch toaster oven-safe baking dish.

2. In a large bowl, add the banana and mash well. Stir in the flaxseed meal, maple syrup, olive oil, cinnamon, vanilla, baking powder, salt, milk, oats, and pecan pieces. Pour mixture into prepared baking dish.

3. Bake oatmeal until the middle is set and browned on the edges, about 25 to 35 minutes. (For softer scoop able oatmeal bake 25 to 30 minutes, for firm oatmeal bake 30 to 35 minutes.)

4. Let sit at least 10 minutes before slicing and serving.

LUNCH RECIPES

Zucchini And Cauliflower Stew

Ingredients:

Servings: 4
Cooking Time:
12 Mins.

- » 1 cauliflower head, florets separated
- » 1 ½ C. zucchinis; sliced
- » 1 handful parsley leaves; chopped.
- » ½ C. tomato puree
- » 2 green onions; chopped.
- » 1 tbsp. balsamic vinegar
- » 1 tbsp. olive oil
- » Salt and black pepper to taste.

Directions:

1. In a pan that fits your air fryer, mix the zucchinis with the rest of the ingredients except the parsley, toss, introduce the pan in the air fryer and cook at 380°F for 20 Mins.
2. Divide into bowls and serve for lunch with parsley sprinkled on top.

Chicken Potato Bake

Ingredients:

Servings: 4
Cooking Time:
25 Mins.

- » 4 potatoes, diced
- » 1 tbsp. garlic, minced
- » 1.5 tbsp. olive oil
- » 1/8 tsp. salt
- » 1/8 tsp. pepper
- » 1.5 lbs. boneless skinless chicken
- » 3/4 C. mozzarella cheese, shredded
- » parsley chopped

Directions:

1. Toss chicken and potatoes with all the spices and oil in a baking pan.
2. Drizzle the cheese on top of the chicken and potato.
3. Press "Power Button" of Air Fry Oven and turn the dial to select the "Bake" mode.
4. Press the Time button and again turn the dial to set the cooking time to 25 minutes.
5. Now push the Temp button and rotate the dial to set the temperature at 375 degrees F.
6. Once preheated, place the baking pan inside and close its lid.
7. Serve warm.

Sweet & Sour Pork

Ingredients:

Servings: 4
Cooking Time:
27 Mins.

» 2 lb. Pork cut into chunks

» 2 large Eggs

» 1 tsp. Pure Sesame Oil (optional)

» 1 C. Potato Starch (or cornstarch)

» 1/2 tsp. Sea Salt

» 1/4 tsp. Freshly Ground Black Pepper

» 1/16 tsp. Chinese Five Spice

» 3 tbsp. Canola Oil

» Oil Mister

Directions:

1. In a mixing bowl, combine salt, potato starch, Chinese Five Spice, and peppers.
2. In another bowl, beat the eggs & add sesame oil.
3. Then dredge the pieces of Pork into the Potato Starch and remove the excess. Then dip each piece into the egg mixture, shake off excess, and then back into the Potato Starch mixture.
4. Place pork pieces into the Instant Pot Duo Crisp Air Fryer Basket after spray the pork with oil.
5. Close the Air Fryer lid and cook at 340°F for approximately 8 to12 minutes (or until pork is cooked), shaking the basket a couple of times for evenly distribution.

Beef Steaks With Beans

Ingredients:

Servings: 4
Cooking Time:
10 Mins.

» 4 beef steaks, trim the fat and cut into strips

» 1 C. green onions, chopped

» 2 cloves garlic, minced

» 1 red bell pepper, seeded and thinly sliced

» 1 can tomatoes, crushed

» 1 can cannellini beans

» 3/4 C. beef broth

» 1/4 tsp. dried basil

» 1/2 tsp. cayenne pepper

» 1/2 tsp. sea salt

» 1/4 tsp. ground black pepper, or to taste

Directions:

1. Preparing the ingredients. Add the steaks, green onions and garlic to the instant crisp air fryer basket.

2. Air frying. Close air fryer lid. Cook at 390 degrees f for 10 minutes, working in batches.

3. Stir in the remaining ingredients and cook for an additional 5 minutes.

Fried Chicken Tacos

Ingredients:

» Chicken
» 1 lb. chicken tenders or breast chopped into 2-inch pieces
» 1 tsp garlic powder
» ½ tsp onion powder
» 1 large egg
» 1 ½ tsp salt
» 1 tsp paprika
» 3 tbsp. buttermilk
» ¾ C. All-purpose flour
» 3 tbsp. corn starch
» ½ tsp black pepper
» ½ tsp cayenne pepper
» oil for spraying

» Coleslaw
» ¼ tsp red pepper flakes
» 2 C. coleslaw mix
» 1 tbsp. brown sugar
» ½ tsp salt
» 2 tbsp. apple cider vinegar
» 1 tbsp. water
» Spicy Mayo
» ½ tsp salt
» ¼ C. mayonnaise
» 1 tsp garlic powder
» 2 tbsp. hot sauce
» 1 tbsp. buttermilk
» Tortilla wrappers

Servings: 4
Cooking Time: 10 Mins.

Directions:

1. Take a large bowl and mix together coleslaw mix, water, brown sugar, salt, apple cider vinegar, and red pepper flakes. Set aside.
2. Take another small bowl and combine mayonnaise, hot sauce, buttermilk, garlic powder, and salt. Set this mixture aside.
3. Select the Instant Pot Duo Crisp Air Fryer option, adjust the temperature to 360°F and push start. Preheating will start.
4. Create a clear station by placing two large flat pans side by side. Whisk together egg and buttermilk with salt and pepper in one of them. In the second, whisk flour, corn starch, black pepper, garlic powder, onion powder, salt, paprika, and cayenne pepper.
5. Cut the chicken tenders into 1-inch pieces. Season all pieces with a little salt and pepper.
6. Once the Instant Pot Duo Crisp Air Fryer is preheated, remove the tray and lightly spray it with oil. Coat your chicken with egg mixture while shaking off any excess egg, followed by the flour mixture, and place it on the tray and tray in the basket, making sure your chicken pieces don't overlap.
7. Close the Air Fryer lid, and cook on 360°F for 10 Mins.
8. while flipping and spraying halfway through cooking.
9. Once the chicken is done, remove and place chicken into warmed tortilla shells. Top with coleslaw and spicy mayonnaise.

Squash And Zucchini Mini Pizza

Ingredients:

Servings: 4
Cooking Time:
15 Mins.

- » 1 pizza crust
- » 1/2 C. parmesan cheese
- » 4 tbsp. oregano
- » 1 zucchini
- » 1 yellow summer squash
- » Olive oil
- » Salt and pepper

Directions:

1. Start by preheating toaster oven to 350°F.
2. If you are using homemade crust, roll out 8 mini portions; if crust is store-bought, use a cookie cutter to cut out the portions.
3. Sprinkle parmesan and oregano equally on each piece. Layer the zucchini and squash in a circle – one on top of the other – around the entire circle.
4. Brush with olive oil and sprinkle salt and pepper to taste.
5. Bake for 15 minutes and serve.

Spicy Avocado Cauliflower Toast

Ingredients:

Servings: 2
Cooking Time: 15 Mins.

- » 1/2 large head of cauliflower, leaves removed
- » 3 1/4 tsp. olive oil
- » 1 small jalapeño
- » 1 tbsp. chopped cilantro leaves
- » 2 slices whole grain bread
- » 1 medium avocado
- » Salt and pepper
- » 5 radishes
- » 1 green onion
- » 2 tsp. hot sauce
- » 1 lime

Directions:

1. Start by preheating toaster oven to 450°F.
2. Cut cauliflower into thick pieces, about 3/4-inches-thick, and slice jalapeño into thin slices.
3. Place cauliflower and jalapeño in a bowl and mix together with 2 tsp. olive oil.
4. Add salt and pepper to taste and mix for another minute.
5. Coat a pan with another tsp. of olive oil, then lay the cauliflower mixture flat across the pan.
6. Cook for 20 minutes, flipping in the last 5 minutes.
7. Reduce heat to toast.
8. Sprinkle cilantro over the mix while it is still warm, and set aside.
9. Brush bread with remaining oil and toast until golden brown, about 5 minutes.
10. Dice onion and radish.
11. Mash avocado in a bowl, then spread on toast and sprinkle salt and pepper to taste.
12. Put cauliflower mix on toast and cover with onion and radish. Drizzle with hot sauce and serve with a lime wedge.

Country Comfort Corn Bread

Ingredients:

Servings: 12
Cooking Time:
20 Mins.

» 1 C. yellow cornmeal

» 1-1/2 C. oatmeal

» 1/4 tsp. salt

» 1/4 C. granulated sugar

» 2 tsp. baking powder

» 1 C. milk

» 1 large egg

» 1/2 C. applesauce

Directions:

1. Start by blending oatmeal into a fine powder.
2. Preheat toaster oven to 400°F.
3. Mix oatmeal, cornmeal, salt, sugar, and baking powder, and stir to blend.
4. Add milk, egg, and applesauce, and mix well.
5. Pour into a pan and bake for 20 minutes.

Air Fried Sausages

Ingredients:

Servings: 6
Cooking Time:
13 Mins.

» 6 sausage

» olive oil spray

Directions:

1. Pour 5 C. of water into Instant Pot Duo Crisp Air Fryer. Place air fryer basket inside the pot, spray inside with nonstick spray and put sausage links inside.
2. Close the Air Fryer lid and steam for about 5 minutes.
3. Remove the lid once done. Spray links with olive oil and close air crisp lid.
4. Set to air crisp at 400°F for 8 min flipping halfway through so both sides get browned.

Cheese-stuffed Meatballs

Ingredients:

Servings: 4
Cooking Time:
10 Mins.

- » ⅓ C. soft bread crumbs
- » 3 tbsp. milk
- » 1 tbsp. ketchup
- » 1 egg
- » ½ tsp. dried marjoram
- » Pinch salt
- » Freshly ground black pepper
- » 1-pound 95 percent lean ground beef
- » 20 ½-inch cubes of cheese
- » Olive oil for misting

Directions:

1. Preparing the ingredients. In a large bowl, combine the bread crumbs, milk, ketchup, egg, marjoram, salt, and pepper, and mix well. Add the ground beef and mix gently but thoroughly with your hands. Form the mixture into 20 meatballs. Shape each meatball around a cheese cube. Mist the meatballs with olive oil and put into the instant crisp air fryer basket.

2. Air frying. Close air fryer lid. Bake for 10 to 13 minutes or until the meatballs register 165°f on a meat thermometer.

Ground Chicken Meatballs

Ingredients:

Servings: 4
Cooking Time:
10 Mins.

» 1-lb. ground chicken

» 1/3 C. panko

» 1 tsp. salt

» 2 tsp. chives

» 1/2 tsp. garlic powder

» 1 tsp. thyme

» 1 egg

Directions:

1. Toss all the meatball Ingredients: in a bowl and mix well.

2. Make small meatballs out this mixture and place them in the air fryer basket.

3. Press "Power Button" of Air Fry Oven and turn the dial to select the "Air Fry" mode.

4. Press the Time button and again turn the dial to set the cooking time to 10 minutes.

5. Now push the Temp button and rotate the dial to set the temperature at 350 degrees F.

6. Once preheated, place the air fryer basket inside and close its lid.

7. Serve warm.

Zingy Dilled Salmon

Ingredients:

- » 2 salmon steaks
- » Coarse sea salt, to taste
- » 1/4 tsp. freshly ground black pepper, or more to taste
- » 1 tbsp. sesame oil
- » Zest of 1 lemon
- » 1 tbsp. fresh lemon juice
- » 1 tsp. garlic, minced
- » 1/2 tsp. smoked cayenne pepper
- » 1/2 tsp. dried dill

Servings: 2
Cooking Time:
20 Mins.

Directions:

1. Preheat your Air Fryer to 380 degrees F. Pat dry the salmon steaks with a kitchen towel.
2. In a ceramic dish, combine the remaining ingredients until everything is well whisked.
3. Add the salmon steaks to the ceramic dish and let them sit in the refrigerator for 1 hour. Now, place the salmon steaks in the cooking basket. Reserve the marinade.
4. Cook for 12 minutes, flipping halfway through the cooking time.
5. Meanwhile, cook the marinade in a small sauté pan over a moderate flame. Cook until the sauce has thickened.
6. Pour the sauce over the steaks and serve.

Greek-style Monkfish With Vegetables

Ingredients:

Servings: 2
Cooking Time: 20 Mins.

- » 2 tsp. olive oil
- » 1 C. celery, sliced
- » 2 bell peppers, sliced
- » 1 tsp. dried thyme
- » 1/2 tsp. dried marjoram
- » 1/2 tsp. dried rosemary
- » 2 monkfish fillets
- » 1 tbsp. soy sauce
- » 2 tbsp. lime juice
- » Coarse salt and ground black pepper, to taste
- » 1 tsp. cayenne pepper
- » 1/2 C. Kalamata olives, pitted and sliced

Directions:

1. In a nonstick skillet, heat the olive oil for 1 minute. Once hot, sauté the celery and peppers until tender, about 4 minutes. Sprinkle with thyme, marjoram, and rosemary and set aside.

2. Toss the fish fillets with the soy sauce, lime juice, salt, black pepper, and cayenne pepper. Place the fish fillets in a lightly greased cooking basket and bake at 390 degrees F for 8 minutes.

3. Turn them over, add the olives, and cook an additional 4 minutes. Serve with the sautéed vegetables on the side.

Filet Mignon With Chili Peanut Sauce

Ingredients:

Servings: 4
Cooking Time: 20 Mins.

- » 2 lb. filet mignon, sliced into bite-sized strips
- » 1 tbsp. oyster sauce
- » 2 tbsp. sesame oil
- » 2 tbsp. tamari sauce
- » 1 tbsp. ginger-garlic paste
- » 1 tbsp. mustard
- » 1 tsp. chili powder
- » 1/4 C. peanut butter
- » 2 tbsp. lime juice
- » 1 tsp. red pepper flakes
- » 2 tbsp. water

Directions:

1. Place the beef strips, oyster sauce, sesame oil, tamari sauce, ginger-garlic paste, mustard, and chili powder in a large ceramic dish.
2. Cover and allow it to marinate for 2 hours in your refrigerator.
3. Cook in the preheated Air Fryer at 400 degrees F for 18 minutes, shaking the basket occasionally.
4. Mix the peanut butter with lime juice, red pepper flakes, and water. Spoon the sauce onto the air fried beef strips and serve warm.

Miso-glazed Salmon

Ingredients:

» 1/4 C. red or white miso

» 1/3 C. sake

» 1 tbsp. soy sauce

» 2 tbsp. vegetable oil

» 1/4 C. sugar

» 4 skinless salmon filets

Directions:

1. In a shallow bowl, mix together the miso, sake, oil, soy sauce, and sugar.

2. Toss the salmon in the mixture until thoroughly coated on all sides.

3. Preheat your toaster oven to "high" on broil mode.

4. Place salmon in a broiling pan and broil until the top is well charred—about 5 minutes.

Lamb Skewers

Ingredients:

» 2 lb. lamb meat; cubed

» 2 red bell peppers; cut into medium pieces

» ¼ C. olive oil

» 2 tbsp. lemon juice

» 1 tbsp. oregano; dried

» 1 tbsp. red vinegar

» 1 tbsp. garlic; minced

» ½ tsp. rosemary; dried

» A pinch of salt and black pepper

Directions:

1. Take a bowl and mix all the ingredients and toss them well.

2. Thread the lamb and bell peppers on skewers, place them in your air fryer's basket and cook at 380°F for 10 minutes on each side. Divide between plates and serve with a side salad

Shrimp Scampi

Ingredients:

» 4 tbsp. salted butter

» 1 lb. shrimp, peeled and deveined

» 2 tbsp. fresh basil, chopped

» 1 tbsp. fresh chives, chopped

» 1 tbsp. fresh lemon juice

» 1 tbsp. garlic, minced

» 2 tsp. red pepper flakes, crushed

» 2 tbsp. dry white wine

**Servings: 6
Cooking Time: 7
Mins.**

Directions:

1. Preheat the Air fryer to 3250F and grease an Air fryer pan.

2. Heat butter, lemon juice, garlic, and red pepper flakes in a pan and return the pan to Air fryer basket.

3. Cook for about 2 minutes and stir in shrimp, basil, chives and wine.

4. Cook for about 5 minutes and dish out the mixture onto serving plates.

5. Serve hot.

Buttered Scallops

Ingredients:

» ¾ lb. sea scallops, cleaned and patted very dry

» 1 tbsp. butter, melted

» ½ tbsp. fresh thyme, minced

» Salt and black pepper, as required

**Servings: 2
Cooking Time: 4
Mins.**

Directions:

1. Preheat the Air fryer to 390 degree F and grease an Air fryer basket.

2. Mix scallops, butter, thyme, salt, and black pepper in a bowl.

3. Arrange scallops in the Air fryer basket and cook for about 4 minutes.

4. Dish out the scallops in a platter and serve hot.

Bacon Pork Bites

Ingredients:

Servings: 6
Cooking Time:
14 Mins.

- » 1-pound pork brisket
- » 6 oz. bacon, sliced
- » 1 tsp. salt
- » 1 tsp. turmeric
- » ½ tsp. red pepper
- » 1 tsp. olive oil
- » 1 tbsp. apple cider vinegar

Directions:

1. Cut the pork brisket into the medium bites.
2. Then put the pork bites in the big mixing bowl.
3. Sprinkle the meat with the turmeric, salt, red pepper, and apple cider vinegar.
4. Mix the pork bites carefully and leave them for 10 minutes to marinate.
5. Then wrap the pork bites in the sliced bacon.
6. Secure the pork bites with the toothpicks.
7. Preheat the air fryer to 370 F.
8. Put the prepared bacon pork bites on the air fryer tray.
9. Cook the pork bites for 8 minutes.
10. After this, turn the pork bites into another side.
11. Cook the dish for 6 minutes more.
12. When the bacon pork bites are cooked – let them in the air fryer for 2 minutes.
13. Then transfer the dish to the serving plate.
14. Enjoy!

Basil Tomatoes

Ingredients:

Servings: 2
Cooking Time: 10 Mins.

» 2 tomatoes, halved

» 1 tbsp. fresh basil, chopped

» Olive oil cooking spray

» Salt and black pepper, as required

Directions:

1. Preheat the Air fryer to 320 degree F and grease an Air fryer basket.
2. Spray the tomato halves evenly with olive oil cooking spray and season with salt, black pepper and basil.
3. Arrange the tomato halves into the Air fryer basket, cut sides up.
4. Cook for about 10 minutes and dish out onto serving plates.

Italian Shrimp Scampi

Ingredients:

Servings: 4
Cooking Time: 20 Mins.

» 2 egg whites

» 1/2 C. coconut flour

» 1 C. Parmigiano-Reggiano, grated

» 1/2 tsp. celery seeds

» 1/2 tsp. porcini powder

» 1/2 tsp. onion powder

» 1 tsp. garlic powder

» 1/2 tsp. dried rosemary

» 1/2 tsp. sea salt

» 1/2 tsp. ground black pepper

» 1 ½ lb. shrimp, deveined

Directions:

1. Whisk the egg with coconut flour and Parmigiano-Reggiano. Add in seasonings and mix to combine well.
2. Dip your shrimp in the batter. Roll until they are covered on all sides.
3. Cook in the preheated Air Fryer at 390 degrees F for 5 to 7 minutes or until golden brown. Work in batches. Serve with lemon wedges if desired.

Crumbly Oat Meatloaf

Ingredients:

Servings: 8
Cooking Time: 60 Mins.

- » 2 lbs. ground beef
- » 1 C. of salsa
- » 3⁄4 C. Quaker Oats
- » 1⁄2 C. chopped onion
- » 1 large egg, beaten
- » 1 tbsp. Worcestershire sauce
- » Salt and black pepper to taste

Directions:

1. Thoroughly mix ground beef with salsa, oats, onion, egg, and all the ingredients in a bowl.
2. Grease a meatloaf pan with oil or butter and spread the minced beef in the pan.
3. Press "Power Button" of Air Fry Oven and turn the dial to select the "Bake" mode.
4. Press the Time button and again turn the dial to set the cooking time to 60 minutes.
5. Now push the Temp button and rotate the dial to set the temperature at 350 degrees F.
6. Once preheated, place the beef baking pan in the oven and close its lid.
7. Slice and serve.

SNACKS AND DESSERTS RECIPES

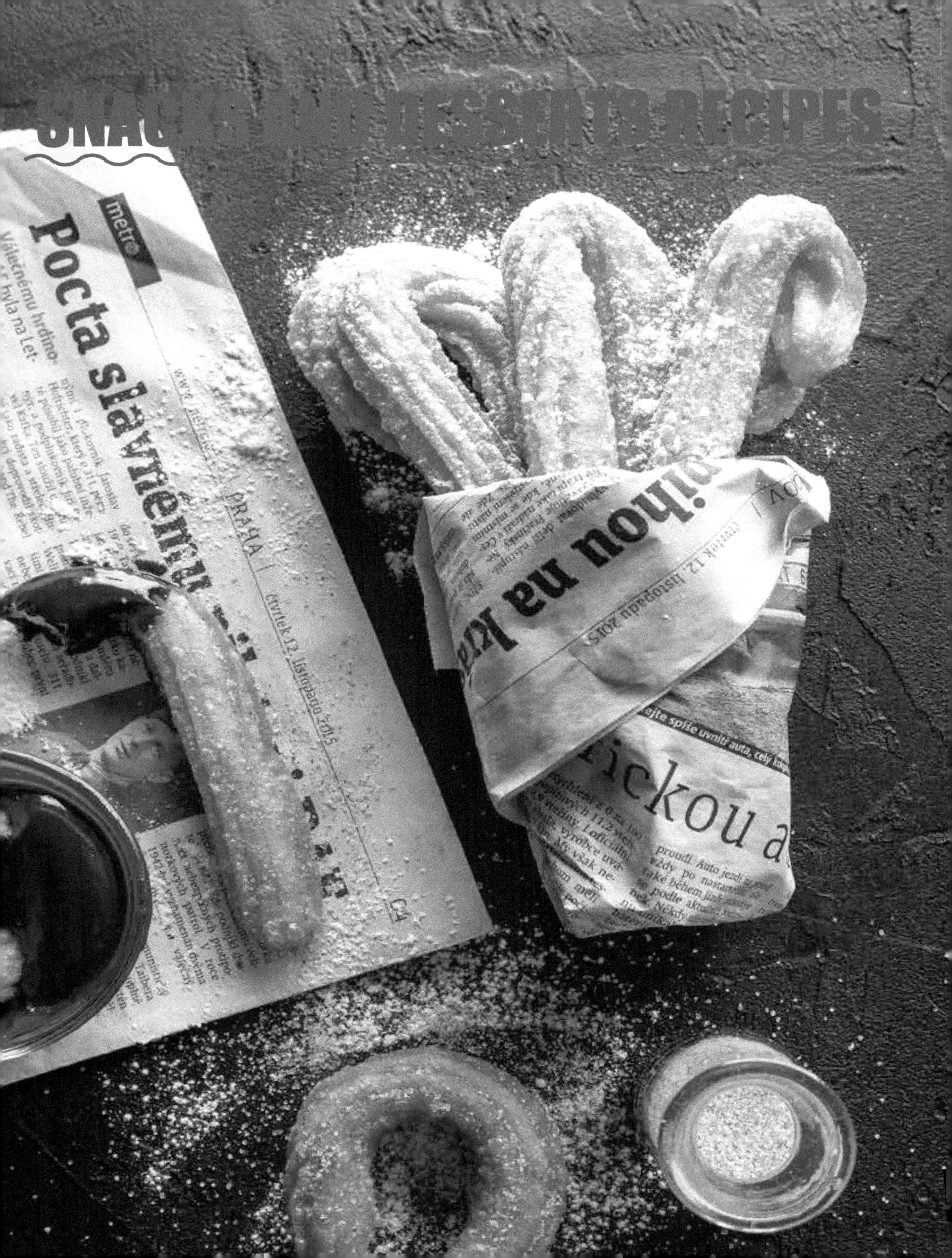

Lemon Bars

Ingredients:

» ½ C. butter, melted

» 1 C. erythritol

» 1 and ¾ C. almond flour

» 3 eggs, whisked

» Zest of 1 lemon, grated

» Juice of 3 lemons

Directions:

1. In a bowl, mix 1 C. flour with half of the erythritol and the butter, stir well and press into a baking dish that fits the air fryer lined with parchment paper.
2. Put the dish in your air fryer and cook at 350 degrees F for 10 minutes.
3. Meanwhile, in a bowl, mix the rest of the flour with the remaining erythritol and the other Ingredients: and whisk well.
4. Spread this over the crust, put the dish in the air fryer once more and cook at 350 degrees F for 25 minutes.
5. Cool down, cut into bars and serve.

Quick Coffee Cake

Ingredients:

» ¼ C. butter

» ½ tsp instant coffee

» 1 tbsp. black coffee, brewed

» 1 egg

» ¼ C. sugar

» ¼ C. flour

» 1 tsp cocoa powder

» Powdered sugar, for icing

Directions:

1. Preheat Cuisinart on Bake function to 330 F. Beat the sugar and egg together in a bowl. Beat in cocoa, instant and black coffees; stir in flour. Transfer the batter to a greased cake pan. Cook for 15 minutes. Dust with powdered sugar and serve.

Chocolate Ramekins

Ingredients:

Servings: 4
Cooking Time: 12 Mins.

» ½ C. butter

» 2/3 C. dark chocolate, chopped

» ¼ C. caster sugar

» 2 medium eggs

» 2 tsp. fresh orange rind, finely grated

» ¼ C. fresh orange juice

» 2 tbsp. self-rising flour

Directions:

1. In a microwave-safe bowl, add the butter, and chocolate and microwave on high heat for about 2 minutes or until melted completely, stirring after every 30 seconds.
2. Remove from microwave and stir the mixture until smooth.
3. Add the sugar, and eggs and whisk until frothy.
4. Add the orange rind and juice, followed by flour and mix until well combined.
5. Divide mixture into 4 greased ramekins about ¾ full.
6. Press "Power Button" of Air Fry Oven and turn the dial to select the "Air Fry" mode.
7. Press the Time button and again turn the dial to set the cooking time to 12 minutes.
8. Now push the Temp button and rotate the dial to set the temperature at 355 degrees F.
9. Press "Start/Pause" button to start.
10. When the unit beeps to show that it is preheated, open the lid.
11. Arrange the ramekins in "Air Fry Basket" and insert in the oven.
12. Place the ramekins set aside to cool completely before serving.

Coconut Cookies With Pecans

Ingredients:

Servings: 10
Cooking Time:
25 Mins.

- » 1½ C. coconut flour
- » 1½ C. extra-fine almond flour
- » ½ tsp. baking powder
- » ½ tsp. baking soda
- » 3 eggs plus an egg yolk, beaten
- » ¾ C. coconut oil, at room temperature
- » 1 C. unsalted pecan nuts, roughly chopped
- » ¾ C. monk fruit
- » ¼ tsp. freshly grated nutmeg
- » ½ tsp. ground cloves
- » ½ tsp. pure vanilla extract
- » ½ tsp. pure coconut extract
- » ⅛ tsp. fine sea salt

Directions:

1. Line the baking pan with parchment paper.
2. Mix the coconut flour, almond flour, baking powder, and baking soda in a large mixing bowl.
3. In another mixing bowl, stir together the eggs and coconut oil. Add the wet mixture to the dry mixture.
4. Mix in the remaining ingredients and stir until a soft dough forms.
5. Drop about 2 tbsp. of dough on the parchment paper for each cookie and flatten each biscuit until it's 1 inch thick.
6. Slide the baking pan into Rack Position 1, select Convection Bake, set temperature to 370ºF (188ºC), and set time to 25 minutes.
7. When cooking is complete, the cookies should be golden and firm to the touch.
8. Remove from the oven to a plate. Let the cookies cool to room temperature and serve.

Roasted Chickpeas

Ingredients:

» 3 C. boiled chickpeas

» ¼ tsp. rosemary

» ¼ tsp. dry mango powder

» 1 tsp. olive oil

» ½ tsp. cinnamon powder

» ¼ tsp. cumin powder

» 1 tsp. salt

» ½ tsp. chili powder

» ¼ tsp. dry coriander powder

Servings: 4
Cooking Time: 10 Mins.

Directions:

1. Preheat your Air Fryer to a temperature of 370°F (190°C).

2. Transfer chickpeas with olive oil in fryer basket and cook for 8 minutes.

3. Shake fryer basket after every 2 minutes.

4. In a bowl add chickpeas with all spices and toss to combine.

5. Serve!

Coffee Chocolate Cake

Ingredients:

Servings: 8
Cooking Time:
30 Mins.

Dry Ingredients:

» 1½ C. almond flour

» ½ C. coconut meal

» ⅔ C. Swerve

» 1 tsp. baking powder

» ¼ tsp. salt

» Wet Ingredients:

» 1 egg

» 1 stick butter, melted

» ½ C. hot strongly brewed coffee

Topping:

» ½ C. confectioner's Swerve

» ¼ C. coconut flour

» 3 tbsp. coconut oil

» 1 tsp. ground cinnamon

» ½ tsp. ground cardamom

Directions:

1. In a medium bowl, combine the almond flour, coconut meal, Swerve, baking powder, and salt.

2. In a large bowl, whisk the egg, melted butter, and coffee until smooth.

3. Add the dry mixture to the wet and stir until well incorporated. Transfer the batter to a greased baking pan.

4. Stir together all the ingredients for the topping in a small bowl. Spread the topping over the batter and smooth the top with a spatula.

5. Slide the baking pan into Rack Position 1, select Convection Bake, set temperature to 330ºF (166ºC), and set time to 30 minutes.

6. When cooking is complete, the cake should spring back when gently pressed with your fingers.

7. Rest for 10 minutes before serving.

Vanilla Rum Cookies With Walnuts

Ingredients:

Servings: 6
Cooking Time:
15 Mins.

- » 1/2 C. almond flour
- » 1/2 C. coconut flour
- » 1/2 tsp. baking powder
- » 1/4 tsp. fine sea salt
- » 1 stick butter, unsalted and softened
- » 1/2 C. swerve
- » 1 egg
- » 1/2 tsp. vanilla
- » 1 tsp. butter rum flavoring
- » 3 oz. walnuts, finely chopped

Directions:

1. Begin by preheating the Air Fryer to 360 degrees F.
2. In a mixing dish, thoroughly combine the flour with baking powder and salt.
3. Beat the butter and swerve with a hand mixer until pale and fluffy; add the whisked egg, vanilla, and butter rum flavoring; mix again to combine well. Now, stir in the dry ingredients.
4. Fold in the chopped walnuts and mix to combine. Divide the mixture into small balls; flatten each ball with a fork and transfer them to a foil-lined baking pan.
5. Bake in the preheated Air Fryer for 14 minutes. Work in a few batches and transfer to wire racks to cool completely.

Easy Air Fryer Tofu

Ingredients:

Servings: 4
Cooking Time: 15 Mins.

» 16 oz extra firm tofu, cut into bite-sized pieces

» 1 tbsp. olive oil

» 1 garlic clove, minced

Directions:

1. Fit the Cuisinart oven with the rack in position 2.
2. Add tofu, garlic, and oil in a mixing bowl and toss well. Let it sit for 15 minutes.
3. Arrange tofu in the air fryer basket then place an air fryer basket in the baking pan.
4. Place a baking pan on the oven rack. Set to air fry at 370 F for 15 minutes.
5. Serve and enjoy.

Apricot Crumble With Blackberries

Ingredients:

Servings: 4
Cooking Time: 30 Mins.

» 2 ½ C. fresh apricots, de-stoned and cubed

» 1 C. fresh blackberries

» ½ C. sugar

» 2 tbsp. lemon Juice

» 1 C. flour

» 5 tbsp. butter

Directions:

1. Preheat Breville on Bake function to 360 F. Add the apricot cubes to a bowl and mix with lemon juice, 2 tbsp. sugar, and blackberries. Scoop the mixture into a greased dish and spread it evenly.
2. In another bowl, mix flour and remaining sugar. Add 1 tbsp. of cold water and butter and keep mixing until you have a crumbly mixture. Pour over the fruit mixture and cook for 20 minutes.

Ultimate Coconut Chocolate Cake

Ingredients:

Servings: 10
Cooking Time:
15 Mins.

» 1¼ C. unsweetened bakers' chocolate

» 1 stick butter

» 1 tsp. liquid stevia

» ⅓ C. shredded coconut

» 2 tbsp. coconut milk

» 2 eggs, beaten

» Cooking spray

Directions:

1. Lightly spritz the baking pan with cooking spray.

2. Place the chocolate, butter, and stevia in a microwave-safe bowl. Microwave for about 30 seconds until melted. Let the chocolate mixture cool to room temperature.

3. Add the remaining ingredients to the chocolate mixture and stir until well incorporated. Pour the batter into the prepared baking pan.

4. Slide the baking pan into Rack Position 1, select Convection Bake, set temperature to 330°F (166°C), and set time to 15 minutes.

5. When cooking is complete, a toothpick inserted in the center should come out clean.

6. Remove from the oven and allow to cool for about 10 minutes before serving.

Honey And Orange Pancakes

Ingredients:

Servings: x
Cooking Time: x

» 2 tsp. dried basil

» 2 tsp. dried parsley

» Salt and Pepper to taste

» 3 tbsp. Butter

» 1 orange (zested)

» 1 ½ C. almond flour

» 3 eggs

» 1 tbsp. honey

Directions:

1. Preheat the air fryer to 250 Fahrenheit.

2. In a small bowl, mix the ingredients together. Ensure that the mixture is smooth and well balanced.

3. Take a pancake mold and grease it with butter. Add the batter to the mold and place it in the air fryer basket.

4. Cook till both the sides of the pancake have browned on both sides and serve with maple syrup.

Baked Beef & Broccoli

Ingredients:

Servings: 2
Cooking Time:
25 Mins.

» 1/2 lb beef meat, cut into pieces

» 1 tbsp. vinegar

» 1 garlic clove, minced

» 1 tbsp. olive oil

» 1/2 tsp Italian seasoning

» 1/2 C. broccoli florets

» 1 onion, sliced

» Pepper

» Salt

Directions:

1. Fit the Cuisinart oven with the rack in position

2. Add meat and remaining ingredients into the large bowl and toss well and spread in baking pan.

3. Set to bake at 390 F for 30 minutes. After 5 minutes place the baking pan in the preheated oven.

4. Serve and enjoy.

Savory Buffalo Chicken

Ingredients:

Servings: 4
Cooking Time:
35 Mins.

» 2 lb. chicken wings

» ½ C. cayenne pepper sauce

» ½ C. coconut oil

» 1 tbsp. Worcestershire sauce

» 1 tbsp. kosher salt

Directions:

1. In a bowl, mix cayenne pepper sauce, coconut oil, Worcestershire sauce, and salt; set aside. Place chicken in the Air Fryer basket and fit in the baking tray. Cook for 25 minutes at 380 F on Air Fy function. Transfer to a large-sized plate and drizzle with the prepared sauce to serve.

Air Fry Chicken Drumsticks

Ingredients:

Servings: 6
Cooking Time:
25 Mins.

» 6 chicken drumsticks

» 1/2 tsp garlic powder

» 2 tbsp. olive oil

» 1/2 tsp ground cumin

» 3/4 tsp paprika

» Pepper

» Salt

Directions:

1. Fit the Cuisinart oven with the rack in position 2.

2. Add chicken drumsticks and olive oil in a large bowl and toss well.

3. Sprinkle garlic powder, paprika, cumin, pepper, and salt over chicken drumsticks and toss until well coated.

4. Place chicken drumsticks in the air fryer basket then place an air fryer basket in the baking pan.

5. Place a baking pan on the oven rack. Set to air fry at 400 F for 25 minutes.

6. Serve and enjoy.

Herb Pork Tenderloin

Ingredients:

Servings: 4
Cooking Time:
35 Mins.

» 1 lb pork tenderloin

» 1/2 tbsp. dried rosemary

» 1/2 tsp dried thyme

» 1 tbsp. olive oil

» Pepper

» Salt

Directions:

1. Fit the Cuisinart oven with the rack in position

2. Mix rosemary, thyme, oil, pepper, and salt and rub over pork tenderloin.

3. Place pork tenderloin in baking pan.

4. Set to bake at 400 F for 40 minutes. After 5 minutes place the baking pan in the preheated oven.

5. Slice and serve.

Pork Sausage With Cauliflower Mash

Ingredients:

Servings: 6
Cooking Time:
27 Mins.

» 1 lb. (454 g) cauliflower, chopped

» 6 pork sausages, chopped

» ½ onion, sliced

» 3 eggs, beaten

» ⅓ C. Colby cheese

» 1 tsp. cumin powder

» ½ tsp. tarragon

» ½ tsp. sea salt

» ½ tsp. ground black pepper

» Cooking spray

Directions:

1. Spritz the baking pan with cooking spray.

2. In a saucepan over medium heat, boil the cauliflower until tender. Place the boiled cauliflower in a food processor and pulse until puréed. Transfer to a large bowl and combine with remaining ingredients until well blended.

3. Pour the cauliflower and sausage mixture into the pan.

4. Slide the baking pan into Rack Position 1, select Convection Bake, set temperature to 365ºF (185ºC) and set time to 27 minutes.

5. When cooking is complete, the sausage should be lightly browned.

6. Divide the mixture among six serving dishes and serve warm.

Chicken Parm

Ingredients:

Servings: 4
Cooking Time:
35 Mins.

» Nonstick cooking spray

» ½ C. flour

» 2 eggs

» 2/3 C. panko bread crumbs

» 2/3 C. Italian seasoned bread crumbs

» 1/3 + ¼ C. parmesan cheese, divided

» 2 tbsp. fresh parsley, chopped

» ½ tsp salt

» ¼ tsp pepper

» 4 chicken breast halves, skinless & boneless

» 24 oz. marinara sauce

» 1 C. mozzarella cheese, grated

Directions:

1. Place the baking pan in position 2 of the oven. Lightly spray the fryer basket with cooking spray.

2. Place flour in a shallow dish.

3. In a separate shallow dish, beat the eggs.

4. In a third shallow dish, combine both bread crumbs, 1/3 C. parmesan cheese, 2 tbsp. parsley, salt, and pepper.

5. Place chicken between two sheets of plastic wrap and lb. to ½-inch thick.

6. Dip chicken first in flour, then eggs, and bread crumb mixture to coat. Place in basket and place the basket on the baking pan.

7. Set oven to air fry on 375°F for 10 minutes. Turn chicken over halfway through cooking time.

8. Remove chicken and baking pan from the oven. Place the rack in position 1. Set oven to bake on 425°F for 30 minutes.

9. Pour 1 ½ C. marinara in the bottom of 8x11-inch baking dish. Place chicken over sauce and add another 2 tbsp. marinara to tops of chicken. Top chicken with mozzarella and parmesan cheese.

10. Once oven preheats for 5 minutes, place the dish in the oven and bake 20-25 minutes until bubbly and cheese is golden brown. Serve.

opycat Taco Bell Crunch Wraps

Ingredients:

Servings: 6
Cooking Time: 2 Mins.

» 6 wheat tostadas

» 2 C. sour cream

» 2 C. Mexican blend cheese

» 2 C. shredded lettuce

» 12 oz. low-sodium nacho cheese

» 3 Roma tomatoes

» 6 12-inch wheat tortillas

» 1 1/3 C. water

» 2 packets low-sodium taco seasoning

» 2 lb. of lean ground beef

Directions:

1. Preparing the Ingredients. Ensure your air fryer oven is preheated to 400 degrees.

2. Make beef according to taco seasoning packets.

3. Place 2/3 C. prepared beef, 4 tbsp. cheese, 1 tostada, 1/3 C. sour cream, 1/3 C. lettuce, 1/6th of tomatoes and 1/3 C. cheese on each tortilla.

4. Fold up tortillas edges and repeat with remaining ingredients.

5. Lay the folded sides of tortillas down into the air fryer oven and spray with olive oil.

6. Air Frying. Set temperature to 400°F, and set time to 2 minutes. Cook 2 minutes till browned.

Salsa Beef Meatballs

Ingredients:

Servings: 4
Cooking Time:
10 Mins.

» 1 lb. (454 g) ground beef (85% lean)

» ½ C. salsa

» ¼ C. diced green or red bell peppers

» 1 large egg, beaten

» ¼ C. chopped onions

» ½ tsp. chili powder

» 1 clove garlic, minced

» ½ tsp. ground cumin

» 1 tsp. fine sea salt

» Lime wedges, for serving

» Cooking spray

Directions:

1. Spritz the air fryer basket with cooking spray.

2. Combine all the ingredients in a large bowl. Stir to mix well.

3. Divide and shape the mixture into 1-inch balls. Arrange the balls in the pan and spritz with cooking spray.

4. Put the air fryer basket on the baking pan and slide into Rack Position 2, select Air Fry, set temperature to 350°F (180°C) and set time to 10 minutes.

5. Flip the balls with tongs halfway through.

6. When cooking is complete, the balls should be well browned.

7. Transfer the balls on a plate and squeeze the lime wedges over before serving.

Cheese Chicken Fries

Ingredients:

Servings: x
Cooking Time: x

» 1 lb. chicken (Cut in to long Oregano Fingers)

» ingredients for the marinade:

» 1 tbsp. olive oil

» 1 tsp. mixed herbs

» ½ tsp. red chili flakes

» A pinch of salt to taste

» 1 tbsp. lemon juice

» For the garnish:

» 1 C. melted cheddar cheese

Directions:

1. Take all the ingredients mentioned under the heading "For the marinade" and mix them well.
2. Cook the chicken Oregano Fingers and soak them in the marinade.
3. Pre heat the Breville smart oven for around 5 minutes at 300 Fahrenheit. Take out the
4. basket of the fryer and place the chicken Oregano Fingers in them. Close the basket.
5. Now keep the fryer at 220 Fahrenheit for 20 or 25 minutes. In between the process, toss the fries twice or thrice so that they get cooked properly.
6. Towards the end of the cooking process (the last 2 minutes or so), sprinkle the cut coriander leaves on the fries. Add the melted cheddar cheese over the fries and serve hot.

Air Fryer Juicy Pork Chops

Ingredients:

Servings: 2
Cooking Time: 12 Mins.

» 2 pork chops

» 2 tbsp. brown sugar

» 1 tbsp. olive oil

» 1/4 tsp garlic powder

» 1/2 tsp onion powder

» 1 tsp ground mustard

» 1 tbsp. paprika

» Pepper

» Salt

Directions:

1. Fit the Cuisinart oven with the rack in position 2.
2. Add all dry ingredients into the small bowl and mix well.
3. Brush pork chops with oil and rub with spice mixture.
4. Place pork chops in the air fryer basket then place an air fryer basket in the baking pan.
5. Place a baking pan on the oven rack. Set to air fry at 400 F for 12 minutes.
6. Serve and enjoy.

Pork Sticks With Red Chili Flakes

Ingredients:

Servings: x
Cooking Time: x

» 2 tsp. salt

» 1 tsp. pepper powder

» 1 tsp. red chili powder

» 2 tsp. red chili flakes

» 1 ½ tbsp. ginger-garlic paste

» 6 tbsp. corn flour

» 4 eggs

» 1 lb. boneless pork cut into Oregano Fingers

» 2 C. dry breadcrumbs

» 2 tsp. oregano

» 4 tbsp. lemon juice

Directions:

1. Mix all the ingredients for the marinade and put the pork Oregano Fingers inside and let it rest overnight. Mix the breadcrumbs, oregano and red chili flakes well and place the marinated Oregano Fingers on this mixture. Cover it with plastic wrap and leave it till right before you serve to cook.

2. Pre heat the Breville smart oven at 160 degrees Fahrenheit for 5 minutes. Place the Oregano Fingers in the fry basket and close it. Let them cook at the same temperature for another 15 minutes or so. Toss the Oregano Fingers well so that they are cooked uniformly.

FISH & SEAFOOD RECIPES

Crispy Paprika Fish Fillets (2)

Ingredients:

» 1/2 C. seasoned breadcrumbs

» 1 tbsp. balsamic vinegar

» 1/2 tsp. seasoned salt

» 1 tsp. paprika

» 1/2 tsp. ground black pepper

» 1 tsp. celery seed

» 2 fish fillets, halved

» 1 egg, beaten

Directions:

1. Preparing the Ingredients. Add the breadcrumbs, vinegar, salt, paprika, ground black pepper, and celery seeds to your food processor. Process for about 30 seconds.

2. Coat the fish fillets with the beaten egg; then, coat them with the breadcrumbs mixture.

3. Air Frying. Cook at 350 degrees F for about 15 minutes.

Old Bay Tilapia Fillets

Ingredients:

» 1 lb. tilapia fillets

» 1 tbsp. old bay seasoning

» 2 tbsp. canola oil

» 2 tbsp. lemon pepper

» Salt to taste

» 2-3 butter buds

Directions:

1. Preheat your Cuisinart oven to 400 F on Bake function. Drizzle tilapia fillets with canola oil. In a bowl, mix salt, lemon pepper, butter buds, and seasoning; spread on the fish. Place the fillet on the basket and fit in the baking tray. Cook for 10 minutes, flipping once until tender and crispy.

Crab Cakes

Ingredients:

» 8 oz. jumbo lump crabmeat

» 1 tbsp. Old Bay Seasoning

» ⅓ C. bread crumbs

» ¼ C. diced red bell pepper

» ¼ C. diced green bell pepper

» 1 egg

» ¼ C. mayonnaise

» Juice of ½ lemon

» 1 tsp. flour

» Cooking oil

Servings: 4
Cooking Time:
10 Mins.

Directions:

1. Preparing the Ingredients. In a large bowl, combine the crabmeat, Old Bay Seasoning, bread crumbs, red bell pepper, green bell pepper, egg, mayo, and lemon juice. Mix gently to combine.

2. Form the mixture into 4 patties. Sprinkle ¼ tsp. of flour on top of each patty.

3. Air Frying. Place the crab cakes in the Cuisinart air fryer oven. Spray them with cooking oil. Cook for 10 minutes.

4. Serve.

Panko Catfish Nuggets

Ingredients:

Servings: 4
Cooking Time:
7 To 8 Mins.

» 2 medium catfish fillets, cut into chunks (approximately 1 × 2 inch)
» Salt and pepper, to taste
» 2 eggs
» 2 tbsp. skim milk
» ½ C. cornstarch
» 1 C. panko bread crumbs
» Cooking spray

Directions:

1. In a medium bowl, season the fish chunks with salt and pepper to taste.
2. In a small bowl, beat together the eggs with milk until well combined.
3. Place the cornstarch and bread crumbs into separate shallow dishes.
4. Dredge the fish chunks one at a time in the cornstarch, coating well on both sides, then dip in the egg mixture, shaking off any excess, finally press well into the bread crumbs. Spritz the fish chunks with cooking spray.
5. Arrange the fish chunks in the air fryer basket in a single layer.
6. Put the air fryer basket on the baking pan and slide into Rack Position 2, select Air Fry, set temperature to 390ºF (199ºC), and set time to 8 minutes.
7. Flip the fish chunks halfway through the cooking time.
8. When cooking is complete, they should be no longer translucent in the center and golden brown. Remove the fish chunks from the oven to a plate. Serve warm.

Fish Spicy Lemon Kebab

Ingredients:

Servings: x
Cooking Time: x

- » 1 lb. boneless fish roughly chopped
- » 3 onions chopped
- » 5 green chilies-roughly chopped
- » 1 ½ tbsp. ginger paste
- » 1 ½ tsp garlic paste
- » 1 ½ tsp salt
- » 3 tsp lemon juice
- » 2 tsp garam masala
- » 4 tbsp. chopped coriander
- » 3 tbsp. cream
- » 2 tbsp. coriander powder
- » 4 tbsp. fresh mint chopped
- » 3 tbsp. chopped capsicum
- » 3 eggs
- » 2 ½ tbsp. white sesame seeds

Directions:

1. Take all the ingredients mentioned under the first heading and mix them in a bowl. Grind them thoroughly to make a smooth paste. Take the eggs in a different bowl and beat them. Add a pinch of salt and leave them aside. Take a flat plate and in it mix the sesame seeds and breadcrumbs. Mold the fish mixture into small balls and flatten them into round and flat kebabs. Dip these kebabs in the egg and salt mixture and then in the mixture of breadcrumbs and sesame seeds. Leave these kebabs in the fridge for an hour or so to set.

2. Pre heat the Breville smart oven at 160 degrees Fahrenheit for around 5 minutes. Place the kebabs in the basket and let them cook for another 25 minutes at the same temperature. Turn the kebabs over in between the cooking process to get a uniform cook. Serve the kebabs with mint sauce.

Crispy Salmon With Lemon-butter Sauce

Ingredients:

Servings: x
Cooking Time: x

» 4 (4-6-oz) salmon fillets, patted dry

» Salt and pepper, to taste

» 2 tbsp. olive oil

» 1 large garlic clove, minced

» 1/3 C. dry white wine

» 2 tbsp. fresh lemon juice

» 1 lemon zested

» 3 tbsp. unsalted butter, diced

» 2 tbsp. chopped fresh dill

Directions:

1. Place Breville smart oven over medium heat.

2. Sprinkle salt and pepper on salmon fillets and add 1 tbsp. oil to the pan.

3. Add salmon flesh side down and cook 3-4 minutes. Flip the salmon and cook an additional 3 minutes on skin side. Transfer to a plate.

4. Wipe out Breville smart oven and add remaining tbsp. olive oil over medium heat.

5. Add garlic and saute for 1 minute.

6. Pour in white wine and lemon juice. Stir for one minute.

7. Add lemon zest and continue stirring until slightly reduced.

8. Reduce heat to low and add cubed butter, stirring after each addition.

9. Sprinkle in fresh dill and stir all together.

10. Season with salt and pepper and pour sauce over salmon fillets.

Cajun Red Snapper

Ingredients:

Servings: 2
Cooking Time:
12 Mins.

» 8 oz red snapper fillets

» 2 tbsp. parmesan cheese, grated

» 1/4 C. breadcrumbs

» 1/2 tsp Cajun seasoning

» 1/4 tsp Worcestershire sauce

» 1 garlic clove, minced

» 1/4 C. butter

Directions:

1. Fit the Cuisinart oven with the rack in position

2. Melt butter in a pan over low heat. Add Cajun seasoning, garlic, and Worcestershire sauce into the melted butter and stir well.

3. Brush fish fillets with melted butter and place into the baking dish.

4. Mix together parmesan cheese and breadcrumbs and sprinkle over fish fillets.

5. Set to bake at 400 F for 17 minutes. After 5 minutes place the baking dish in the preheated oven.

6. Serve and enjoy.

Parmesan Fish Fillets

Ingredients:

Servings: 4
Cooking Time:
17 Mins.

» ⅓ C. grated Parmesan cheese

» ½ tsp. fennel seed

» ½ tsp. tarragon

» ⅓ tsp. mixed peppercorns

» 2 eggs, beaten

» 4 (4-ounce / 113-g) fish fillets, halved

» 2 tbsp. dry white wine

» 1 tsp. seasoned salt

Directions:

1. Place the grated Parmesan cheese, fennel seed, tarragon, and mixed peppercorns in a food processor and pulse for about 20 seconds until well combined. Transfer the cheese mixture to a shallow dish.
2. Place the beaten eggs in another shallow dish.
3. Drizzle the dry white wine over the top of fish fillets. Dredge each fillet in the beaten eggs on both sides, shaking off any excess, then roll them in the cheese mixture until fully coated. Season with the salt.
4. Arrange the fillets in the air fryer basket.
5. Put the air fryer basket on the baking pan and slide into Rack Position 2, select Air Fry, set temperature to 345ºF (174ºC), and set time to 17 minutes.
6. Flip the fillets once halfway through the cooking time.
7. When cooking is complete, the fish should be cooked through no longer translucent. Remove from the oven and cool for 5 minutes before serving.

Baked Spinach Tilapia

Ingredients:

Servings: 4
Cooking Time:
10 Mins.

» 1 lb tilapia fillets

» 1 C. Monterey jack cheese, shredded

» 3 tbsp. butter, sliced

» 8 oz spinach

Directions:

1. Fit the Cuisinart oven with the rack in position

2. Add spinach into the baking dish and top with butter slices.

3. Place fish fillets on top of spinach.

4. Sprinkle shredded cheese over fish fillets.

5. Set to bake at 450 F for 15 minutes. After 5 minutes place the baking dish in the preheated oven.

6. Serve and enjoy.

Lobster Tails With Lemon-garlic Sauce

Ingredients:

Servings: 4
Cooking Time:
15 Mins.

» 1 lb lobster tails

» 1 garlic clove, minced

» 1 tbsp. butter

» Salt and black pepper to taste

» ½ tbsp. lemon Juice

Directions:

1. Add all the ingredients to a food processor, except for lobster and blend well. Wash lobster and halve using meat knife; clean the skin of the lobster and cover with the marinade.

2. Preheat your Breville to 380 F. Place the lobster in the cooking basket and press Start. Cook for 10 minutes on AirFry function. Serve with fresh herbs.

aked Spinach Tilapia

Ingredients:

» 1 lb tilapia fillets

» 1 C. Monterey jack cheese, shredded

» 3 tbsp. butter, sliced

» 8 oz spinach

Directions:

1. Fit the Cuisinart oven with the rack in position

2. Add spinach into the baking dish and top with butter slices.

3. Place fish fillets on top of spinach.

4. Sprinkle shredded cheese over fish fillets.

5. Set to bake at 450 F for 15 minutes. After 5 minutes place the baking dish in the preheated oven.

6. Serve and enjoy.

Saucy Cod With Green Onions

Ingredients:

» 4 cod fillets

» 2 tbsp. fresh cilantro, chopped

» Salt to taste

» 4 green onions, chopped

» 5 slices of ginger, chopped

» 5 tbsp. soy sauce

» 3 tbsp. oil

» 5 rock sugar cubes

Directions:

1. Preheat Breville on AirFry function to 390 F. Season the cod with salt and coriander and drizzle with some olive oil. Place the fish fillet in the basket and press Start. Cook for 15 minutes.

2. Heat the remaining olive oil in a skillet over medium heat and sauté green onions and ginger for 3 minutes. Add in the remaining ingredients and 1 C. of water. Bring to a boil and cook for 5 minutes until the sauce thickens. Pour the sauce over the fish and serve.

Paprika Cauliflower

Ingredients:

Servings: 4
Cooking Time:
20 Mins.

» 1 large head cauliflower, broken into small florets

» 2 tsp. smoked paprika

» 1 tsp. garlic powder

» Salt and freshly ground black pepper, to taste

» Cooking spray

Directions:

1. Spray the air fryer basket with cooking spray.
2. In a medium bowl, toss the cauliflower florets with the smoked paprika and garlic powder until evenly coated. Sprinkle with salt and pepper.
3. Place the cauliflower florets in the basket and lightly mist with cooking spray.
4. Put the air fryer basket on the baking pan and slide into Rack Position 2, select Air Fry, set temperature to 400ºF (205ºC), and set time to 20 minutes.
5. Stir the cauliflower four times during cooking.
6. Remove the cauliflower from the oven and serve hot.

Roasted Butternut Squash With Maple Syrup

Ingredients:

Servings: 4
Cooking Time:
30 Mins.

» 1 lb butternut squash

» 1 tsp dried rosemary

» 2 tbsp. maple syrup

» Salt to taste

Directions:

1. Place the squash on a cutting board and peel. Cut in half and remove the seeds and pulp. Slice into wedges and season with salt. Spray with cooking spray and sprinkle with rosemary.
2. Preheat Breville on AirFry function to 350 F. Transfer the wedges to the greased basket without overlapping. Press Start and cook for 20 minutes. Serve drizzled with maple syrup.

Cauliflower Gnocchi's

Ingredients:

Servings: x
Cooking Time: x

» 2 tbsp. oil

» 2 tsp. ginger-garlic paste

» 2 tsp. soya sauce

» 2 tsp. vinegar

» 1 ½ C. all-purpose flour

» ½ tsp. salt

» 5 tbsp. water

» 2 C. grated cauliflower

Directions:

1. Squeeze the dough and cover it with plastic wrap and set aside. Next, cook the ingredients for the filling and try to ensure that the cauliflower is covered well with the sauce.

2. Roll the dough and place the filling in the center. Now, wrap the dough to cover the filling and pinch the edges together.

3. Pre heat the Breville smart oven at 200° F for 5 minutes. Place the gnocchi's in the fry basket and close it. Let them cook at the same temperature for another 20

4. minutes. Recommended sides are chili sauce or ketchup.

Rosemary Roasted Squash With Cheese

Ingredients:

» 1 lb. (454 g) butternut squash, cut into wedges

» 2 tbsp. olive oil

» 1 tbsp. dried rosemary

» Salt, to salt

» 1 C. crumbled goat cheese

» 1 tbsp. maple syrup

Servings: 2
Cooking Time:
20 Mins.

Directions:

1. Toss the squash wedges with the olive oil, rosemary, and salt in a large bowl until well coated.

2. Transfer the squash wedges to the air fryer basket, spreading them out in as even a layer as possible.

3. Put the air fryer basket on the baking pan and slide into Rack Position 2, select Air Fry, set temperature to 350°F (180°C), and set time to 20 minutes.

4. After 10 minutes, remove from the oven and flip the squash. Return the pan to the oven and continue cooking for 10 minutes.

5. When cooking is complete, the squash should be golden brown. Remove from the oven. Sprinkle the goat cheese on top and serve drizzled with the maple syrup.

Black Gram French Cuisine Galette

Ingredients:

Servings: x
Cooking Time: x

» 2 or 3 green chilies finely chopped

» 1 ½ tbsp. lemon juice

» Salt and pepper to taste

» 2 C. black gram

» 2 medium potatoes boiled and mashed

» 1 ½ C. coarsely crushed peanuts

» 3 tsp. ginger finely chopped

» 1-2 tbsp. fresh coriander leaves

Directions:

1. Mix the ingredients in a clean bowl.

2. Mold this mixture into round and flat French Cuisine Galettes.

3. Wet the French Cuisine Galettes slightly with water.

4. Pre heat the Breville smart oven at 160 degrees Fahrenheit for 5 minutes. Place the French Cuisine Galettes in the fry basket and let them cook for another 25 minutes at the same temperature. Keep rolling them over to get a uniform cook. Serve either with mint sauce or ketchup.

Chili Cottage Cheese

Ingredients:

Servings: x
Cooking Time: x

- » 2 tbsp. olive oil
- » 1 capsicum. Cut into thin and long pieces (lengthwise).
- » 2 small onions. Cut them into halves.
- » 1 ½ tsp. ginger garlic paste.
- » ½ tbsp. red chili sauce.
- » 2 tbsp. tomato ketchup.
- » 1 ½ tbsp. sweet chili sauce.
- » 2 tsp. vinegar.
- » 2 tsp. soya sauce.
- » A few drops of edible red food coloring.
- » 1-2 tbsp. honey.
- » 2 C. cubed cottage cheese
- » 2 ½ tsp. ginger-garlic paste
- » 1 tsp. red chili sauce
- » ¼ tsp. salt
- » ¼ tsp. red chili powder/black pepper
- » A few drops of edible orange food coloring
- » ¼ tsp. Ajinomoto.
- » A pinch of black pepper powder.
- » 1-2 tsp. red chili flakes.
- » For the garnish, use the greens of spring onions and sesame seeds.

Directions:

1. Create the mix for the cottage cheese cubes and coat the chicken well with it.
2. Pre heat the Breville smart oven at 250 Fahrenheit for 5 minutes or so. Open the basket of the Fryer. Place the Oregano Fingers inside the basket. Now let the fryer stay at 290 Fahrenheit for another 20 minutes. Keep tossing the Oregano Fingers periodically through the cook to get a uniform cook.
3. Add the ingredients to the sauce and cook it with the vegetables till it thickens. Add the Oregano Fingers to the sauce and cook till the flavors have blended.

Mushroom Marinade Cutlet

Ingredients:

Servings: x
Cooking Time: x

- » 2 C. fresh green coriander
- » ½ C. mint leaves
- » 4 tsp. fennel
- » 2 tbsp. ginger-garlic paste
- » 1 small onion
- » 6-7 flakes garlic (optional)
- » Salt to taste
- » 2 C. sliced mushrooms
- » 1 big capsicum (Cut this capsicum into big cubes)
- » 1 onion (Cut it into quarters. Now separate the layers carefully.)
- » 5 tbsp. gram flour
- » A pinch of salt to taste
- » 3 tbsp. lemon juice

Directions:

1. Take a clean and dry container. Put into it the coriander, mint, fennel, and ginger, onion/garlic, salt and lemon juice. Mix them.
2. Pour the mixture into a grinder and blend until you get a thick paste. Slit the mushroom almost till the end and leave them aside. Now stuff all the pieces with the paste and set aside. Take the sauce and add to it the gram flour and some salt. Mix them together properly. Rub this mixture all over the stuffed mushroom.
3. Now, to the leftover sauce, add the capsicum and onions. Apply the sauce generously on each of the pieces of capsicum and onion. Now take satay sticks and arrange the cottage cheese pieces and vegetables on separate sticks.
4. Pre heat the Breville smart oven at 290 Fahrenheit for around 5 minutes. Open the basket. Arrange the satay sticks properly. Close the basket. Keep the sticks with the mushroom at 180 degrees for around half an hour while the sticks with the vegetables are to be kept at the same temperature for only 7 minutes. Turn the sticks in between so that one side does not get burnt and also to provide a uniform cook.

Carrot & Chickpea Oat Balls With Cashews

Ingredients:

Servings: 4
Cooking Time:
30 Mins.

» 2 tbsp. olive oil

» 2 tbsp. soy sauce

» 1 tbsp. flax meal

» 2 C. canned chickpeas, drained

» ½ C. sweet onions, diced

» ½ C. carrots, grated

» ½ C. cashews, toasted

» Juice of 1 lemon

» ½ tsp turmeric

» 1 tsp cumin

» 1 tsp garlic powder

» 1 C. rolled oats

Directions:

1. Preheat Breville on AirFry function to 380 F. Heat olive oil in a skillet and sauté onions and carrots for 5 minutes. Ground the oats and cashews in a food processor. Transfer to a bowl.

2. Place the chickpeas, lemon juice, and soy sauce in the food processor and process until smooth. Add them to the bowl as well. Mix in the onions and carrots.

3. Stir in the remaining ingredients until fully incorporated. Make balls out of the mixture. Place them in the frying basket and press Start. Cook for 12 minutes. Serve warm.

Potato Club Barbeque Sandwich

Ingredients:

Servings: x
Cooking Time: x

» ½ flake garlic crushed

» ¼ C. chopped onion

» ¼ tbsp. red chili sauce

» 2 slices of white bread

» 1 tbsp. softened butter

» 1 C. boiled potato

» 1 small capsicum

» ¼ tbsp. Worcestershire sauce

» ½ tsp. olive oil

Directions:

1. Take the slices of bread and remove the edges. Now cut the slices horizontally.

2. Cook the ingredients for the sauce and wait till it thickens. Now, add the potato to the sauce and stir till it obtains the flavors. Roast the capsicum and peel the skin off. Cut the capsicum into slices. Mix the ingredients together and apply it to the bread slices.

3. Pre-heat the Breville smart oven for 5 minutes at 300 Fahrenheit. Open the basket of the Fryer and place the prepared Classic Sandwiches in it such that no two Classic Sandwiches are touching each other. Now keep the fryer at 250 degrees for around 15 minutes. Turn the Classic Sandwiches in between the cooking process to cook both slices. Serve the Classic Sandwiches with tomato ketchup or mint sauce.

Parmesan Breaded Zucchini Chips

Ingredients:

Servings: 5
Cooking Time: 20 Mins.

For the zucchini chips:

» 2 medium zucchini

» 2 eggs

» ⅓ C. bread crumbs

» ⅓ C. grated Parmesan cheese

» Salt

» Pepper

» Cooking oil

For the lemon aioli:

» ½ C. mayonnaise

» ½ tbsp. olive oil

» Juice of ½ lemon

» 1 tsp. minced garlic

» Salt

» Pepper

Directions:

1. Preparing the Ingredients. To make the zucchini chips:
2. Slice the zucchini into thin chips (about ⅛ inch thick) using a knife or mandoline.
3. In a small bowl, beat the eggs. In another small bowl, combine the bread crumbs, Parmesan cheese, and salt and pepper to taste.
4. Spray the Oven rack/basket with cooking oil.
5. Dip the zucchini slices one at a time in the eggs and then the bread crumb mixture. You can also sprinkle the bread crumbs onto the zucchini slices with a spoon.
6. Place the zucchini chips in the Oven rack/basket, but do not stack. Place the Rack on the middle-shelf of the Cuisinart air fryer oven.
7. Air Frying. Cook in batches. Spray the chips with cooking oil from a distance (otherwise, the breading may fly off). Cook for 10 minutes.
8. Remove the cooked zucchini chips from the air fryer oven, then repeat step 5 with the remaining zucchini.
9. To make the lemon aioli:
10. While the zucchini is cooking, combine the mayonnaise, olive oil, lemon juice, and garlic in a small bowl, adding salt and pepper to taste. Mix well until fully combined.
11. Cool the zucchini and serve alongside the aioli.

Cottage Cheese Fingers

Ingredients:

Servings: x
Cooking Time: x

- » 2 tsp. salt
- » 1 tsp. pepper powder
- » 1 tsp. red chili powder
- » 6 tbsp. corn flour
- » 4 eggs
- » 2 C. cottage cheese Oregano Fingers
- » 2 C. dry breadcrumbs
- » 2 tsp. oregano
- » 1 ½ tbsp. ginger-garlic paste
- » 4 tbsp. lemon juice

Directions:

1. Mix all the ingredients for the marinade and put the chicken Oregano Fingers inside and let it rest overnight.
2. Mix the breadcrumbs, oregano and red chili flakes well and place the marinated Oregano Fingers on this mixture. Cover it with plastic wrap and leave it till right before you serve to cook.
3. Pre heat the Breville smart oven at 160 degrees Fahrenheit for 5 minutes. Place the Oregano Fingers in the fry basket and close it. Let them cook at the same temperature for another 15 minutes or so. Toss the Oregano Fingers well so that they are cooked uniformly.

Mashed Turnips

Ingredients:

Servings: 4
Cooking Time: 5 Mins.

- » ½ C. chicken stock
- » 4 turnips, peeled and chopped
- » ¼ C. sour cream
- » Salt and ground black pepper, to taste
- » 1 yellow onion, peeled and chopped

Directions:

1. In the Instant Pot, mix the turnips with the stock and onion. Stir, cover and cook in manual setting for 5 minutes.
2. Release the pressure naturally, drain the turnips and transfer to a bowl. Mix them using a food processor and add salt and pepper to taste and sour cream. Mix again and serve.

Herbed Radish Sauté (2)

Ingredients:

Servings: 4
Cooking Time: 20 Mins.

- » 2 bunches red radishes; halved
- » 2 tbsp. parsley; chopped.
- » 2 tbsp. balsamic vinegar
- » 1 tbsp. olive oil
- » Salt and black pepper to taste.

Directions:

1. Take a bowl and mix the radishes with the remaining ingredients except the parsley, toss and put them in your air fryer's basket.
2. Cook at 400°F for 15 minutes, divide between plates, sprinkle the parsley on top and serve as a side dish

Honey Corn Muffins

Ingredients:

Servings: 8
Cooking Time:
20 Mins.

» 2 eggs

» 1/2 C. sugar

» 1 1/4 C. self-rising flour

» 3/4 C. yellow cornmeal

» 1/2 C. butter, melted

» 3/4 C. buttermilk

» 1 tbsp. honey

Directions:

1. Fit the Cuisinart oven with the rack in position

2. Spray 8-cups muffin tin with cooking spray and set aside.

3. In a large bowl, mix together cornmeal, sugar, and flour.

4. In a separate bowl, whisk the eggs with buttermilk and honey until well combined.

5. Slowly add egg mixture and melted butter to the cornmeal mixture and stir until just mixed.

6. Spoon batter into the prepared muffin tin.

7. Set to bake at 350 F for 25 minutes. After 5 minutes place muffin tin in the preheated oven.

8. Serve and enjoy.

Cheesy Broccoli Gratin

Ingredients:

» ⅓ C. fat-free milk

» 1 tbsp. all-purpose or gluten-free flour

» ½ tbsp. olive oil

» ½ tsp. ground sage

» ¼ tsp. kosher salt

» ⅛ tsp. freshly ground black pepper

» 2 C. roughly chopped broccoli florets

» 6 tbsp. shredded Cheddar cheese

» 2 tbsp. panko bread crumbs

» 1 tbsp. grated Parmesan cheese

» Olive oil spray

Servings: 2
Cooking Time:
14 Mins.

Directions:

1. Spritz the baking pan with olive oil spray.

2. Mix the milk, flour, olive oil, sage, salt, and pepper in a medium bowl and whisk to combine. Stir in the broccoli florets, Cheddar cheese, bread crumbs, and Parmesan cheese and toss to coat.

3. Pour the broccoli mixture into the prepared baking pan.

4. Slide the baking pan into Rack Position 1, select Convection Bake, set temperature to 330°F (166°C), and set time to 14 minutes.

5. When cooking is complete, the top should be golden brown and the broccoli should be tender. Remove from the oven and serve immediately.

Roasted Beets With Grapefruit Glaze

Ingredients:

Servings: 5
Cooking Time:
10 Mins.

» 3 lb. beets

» 1 C. fresh-squeezed grapefruit juice (approximately 2 medium grapefruits)

» 1 tbsp. rice vinegar

» 3 scant tbsp. pure maple syrup

» 1 tbsp. corn starch

Directions:

1. Start by preheating toaster oven to 450°F. Place beets in a roasting pan and sprinkle with water.

2. Roast beets until soft enough to be pierced with a fork, at least 40 minutes.

3. Remove beets and allow to cool until you can handle them.

4. Peel skin off beets and thinly slice.

5. Mix together grapefruit juice, syrup, and vinegar in a small bowl.

6. Pour corn starch into a medium sauce pan and slowly add grapefruit mixture. Stir together until there are no clumps.

7. Heat sauce to a light boil then reduce heat and simmer for 5 minutes, stirring often.

8. Drizzle glaze over beets and serve.

Cheddar Tortilla Chips

Ingredients:

» 1 C. flour

» Salt and black pepper to taste

» 1 tbsp. golden flaxseed meal

» 2 C. shredded Cheddar cheese

Directions:

1. Melt cheddar cheese in the microwave for 1 minute. Once melted, add the flour, salt, flaxseed meal, and pepper. Mix well with a fork.

2. On a board, place the dough and knead it with hands while warm until the ingredients are well combined. Divide the dough into 2 and with a rolling pin, roll them out flat into 2 rectangles.

3. Use a pastry cutter to cut out triangle-shaped pieces and line them in a single layer on a baking dish without touching or overlapping; spray with cooking spray.

4. Select AirFry function, adjust the temperature to 380 F, and press Start. Cook for 10 minutes. Serve with tomato sauce.

Air Fried Eggplant Cubes

Ingredients:

» 1 eggplant, cut into cubes

» 1/4 tsp oregano

» 1 tbsp. olive oil

» 1/2 tsp garlic powder

Directions:

1. Fit the Cuisinart oven with the rack in position 2.

2. Add all ingredients into the large bowl and toss well.

3. Transfer eggplant into in air fryer basket then places the air fryer basket in the baking pan.

4. Place a baking pan on the oven rack. Set to air fry at 390 F for 12 minutes.

5. Serve and enjoy.

Herb Balsamic Mushrooms

Ingredients:

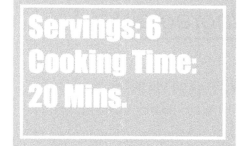

Servings: 6
Cooking Time:
20 Mins.

- » 1 lb button mushrooms, scrubbed and stems trimmed
- » 2 tbsp. olive oil
- » 4 tbsp. balsamic vinegar
- » 1/2 tsp dried basil
- » 1/2 tsp dried oregano
- » 3 garlic cloves, crushed
- » 1/4 tsp black pepper
- » 1 tsp sea salt

Directions:

1. Fit the Cuisinart oven with the rack in position
2. In a large bowl, whisk together vinegar, basil, oregano, garlic, olive oil, pepper, and salt. Stir in mushrooms and let sit for 15 minutes.
3. Spread mushrooms in baking pan.
4. Set to bake at 425 F for 25 minutes. After 5 minutes place the baking pan in the preheated oven.
5. Serve and enjoy.

Spicy Brussels Sprouts (2)

Ingredients:

Servings: 4
Cooking Time:
15 Mins.

- » 1 lb Brussels sprouts, cut in half
- » 1 1/2 tbsp. olive oil
- » 1 tbsp. gochujang
- » 1/2 tsp salt

Directions:

1. Fit the Cuisinart oven with the rack in position 2.
2. In a large mixing bowl, mix together olive oil, gochujang, and salt.
3. Add Brussels sprouts into the bowl and toss until well coated.
4. Transfer Brussels sprouts in air fryer basket then place air fryer basket in baking pan.
5. Place a baking pan on the oven rack. Set to air fry at 360 F for 20 minutes.
6. Serve and enjoy.

Buttered Corn

Ingredients:

Servings: 4
Cooking Time:
20 Mins.

» 2 corn on the cob

» Salt and freshly ground black pepper, as needed

» 2 tbsp. butter, softened and divided

Directions:

1. Sprinkle the cobs evenly with salt and black pepper.

2. Then, rub with 1 tbsp. of butter.

3. With 1 piece of foil, wrap each cob.

4. Press "Power Button" of Air Fry Oven and turn the dial to select the "Air Fry" mode.

5. Press the Time button and again turn the dial to set the cooking time to 20 minutes.

6. Now push the Temp button and rotate the dial to set the temperature at 320 degrees F.

7. Press "Start/Pause" button to start.

8. When the unit beeps to show that it is preheated, open the lid.

9. Arrange the cobs in "Air Fry Basket" and insert in the oven.

10. Serve warm.

Rosemary Roasted Potatoes

Ingredients:

Servings: 4
Cooking Time: 20 Mins.

» 1½ lb. (680 g) small red potatoes, cut into 1-inch cubes

» 2 tbsp. olive oil

» 2 tbsp. minced fresh rosemary

» 1 tbsp. minced garlic

» 1 tsp. salt, plus additional as needed

» ½ tsp. freshly ground black pepper, plus additional as needed

Directions:

1. Toss the potato cubes with the olive oil, rosemary, garlic, salt, and pepper in a large bowl until thoroughly coated.

2. Arrange the potato cubes in the air fryer basket in a single layer.

3. Put the air fryer basket on the baking pan and slide into Rack Position 2, select Roast, set temperature to 400°F (205°C), and set time to 20 minutes.

4. Stir the potatoes a few times during cooking for even cooking.

5. When cooking is complete, the potatoes should be tender. Remove from the oven to a plate. Taste and add additional salt and pepper as needed.

Lush Seafood Casserole

Ingredients:

Servings: 2
Cooking Time: 22 Mins.

- » 1 tbsp. olive oil
- » 1 small yellow onion, chopped
- » 2 garlic cloves, minced
- » 4 oz. (113 g) tilapia pieces
- » 4 oz. (113 g) rockfish pieces
- » ½ tsp. dried basil
- » Salt and ground white pepper, to taste
- » 4 eggs, lightly beaten
- » 1 tbsp. dry sherry
- » 4 tbsp. cheese, shredded

Directions:

1. Heat the olive oil in a nonstick skillet over medium-high heat until shimmering.
2. Add the onion and garlic and sauté for 2 minutes or until fragrant.
3. Add the tilapia, rockfish, basil, salt, and white pepper to the skillet. Sauté to combine well and transfer them into the baking pan.
4. Combine the eggs, sherry and cheese in a large bowl. Stir to mix well. Pour the mixture in the baking pan over the fish mixture.
5. Slide the baking pan into Rack Position 1, select Convection Bake, set temperature to 360°F (182°C) and set time to 20 minutes.
6. When cooking is complete, the eggs should be set and the casserole edges should be lightly browned.
7. Serve immediately.

Parsnip Fries With Garlic-yogurt Dip

Ingredients:

Servings: 4
Cooking Time:
10 Mins.

» 3 medium parsnips, peeled, cut into sticks

» ¼ tsp. kosher salt

» 1 tsp. olive oil

» 1 garlic clove, unpeeled

» Cooking spray

Dip:

» ¼ C. plain Greek yogurt

» ⅛ tsp. garlic powder

» 1 tbsp. sour cream

» ¼ tsp. kosher salt

» Freshly ground black pepper, to taste

Directions:

1. Spritz the air fryer basket with cooking spray.

2. Put the parsnip sticks in a large bowl, then sprinkle with salt and drizzle with olive oil.

3. Transfer the parsnip into the basket and add the garlic.

4. Put the air fryer basket on the baking pan and slide into Rack Position 2, select Air Fry, set temperature to 360°F (182°C) and set time to 10 minutes.

5. Stir the parsnip halfway through the cooking time.

6. Meanwhile, peel the garlic and crush it. Combine the crushed garlic with the ingredients for the dip. Stir to mix well.

7. When cooked, the parsnip sticks should be crisp. Remove the parsnip fries from the oven and serve with the dipping sauce.

Southwest Corn And Bell Pepper Roast

Ingredients:

Corn:

» 1½ C. thawed frozen corn kernels

» 1 C. mixed diced bell peppers

» 1 jalapeño, diced

» 1 C. diced yellow onion

» ½ tsp. ancho chile powder

» 1 tbsp. fresh lemon juice

» 1 tsp. ground cumin

» ½ tsp. kosher salt

» Cooking spray

For Serving:

» ¼ C. feta cheese

» ¼ C. chopped fresh cilantro

» 1 tbsp. fresh lemon juice

Directions:

1. Spritz the air fryer basket with cooking spray.
2. Combine the ingredients for the corn in a large bowl. Stir to mix well.
3. Pour the mixture into the basket.
4. Put the air fryer basket on the baking pan and slide into Rack Position 2, select Air Fry, set temperature to 375ºF (190ºC) and set time to 10 minutes.
5. Stir the mixture halfway through the cooking time.
6. When done, the corn and bell peppers should be soft.
7. Transfer them onto a large plate, then spread with feta cheese and cilantro. Drizzle with lemon juice and serve.

Roasted Mushrooms

Ingredients:

Servings: 1½
Cooking Time:
30 Mins.

» 1 lb. (454 g) button or cremini mushrooms, washed, stems trimmed, and cut into quarters or thick slices

» ¼ C. water

» 1 tsp. kosher salt or ½ tsp. fine salt

» 3 tbsp. unsalted butter, cut into pieces, or extra-virgin olive oil

Directions:

1. Place a large piece of aluminum foil on the sheet pan. Place the mushroom pieces in the middle of the foil. Spread them out into an even layer. Pour the water over them, season with the salt, and add the butter. Wrap the mushrooms in the foil.

2. Select Roast, set the temperature to 325°F (163°C), and set the time for 15 minutes. Select Start to begin preheating.

3. Once the unit has preheated, place the pan in the oven.

4. After 15 minutes, remove the pan from the oven. Transfer the foil packet to a cutting board and carefully unwrap it. Pour the mushrooms and cooking liquid from the foil onto the sheet pan.

5. Select Roast, set the temperature to 350°F (180°C), and set the time for 15 minutes. Return the pan to the oven. Select Start to begin.

6. After about 10 minutes, remove the pan from the oven and stir the mushrooms. Return the pan to the oven and continue cooking for anywhere from 5 to 15 more minutes, or until the liquid is mostly gone and the mushrooms start to brown.

7. Serve immediately.

Classic Worcestershire Poutine

Ingredients:

Servings: 2
Cooking Time:
33 Mins.

- » 2 russet potatoes, scrubbed and cut into ½-inch sticks
- » 2 tsp. vegetable oil
- » 2 tbsp. butter
- » ¼ onion, minced
- » ¼ tsp. dried thyme
- » 1 clove garlic, smashed
- » 3 tbsp. all-purpose flour
- » 1 tsp. tomato paste
- » 1½ C. beef stock
- » 2 tsp. Worcestershire sauce
- » Salt and freshly ground black pepper, to taste
- » ⅔ C. chopped string cheese

Directions:

1. Bring a pot of water to a boil, then put in the potato sticks and blanch for 4 minutes.
2. Drain the potato sticks and rinse under running cold water, then pat dry with paper towels.
3. Transfer the sticks in a large bowl and drizzle with vegetable oil. Toss to coat well. Place the potato sticks in the air fryer basket.
4. Put the air fryer basket on the baking pan and slide into Rack Position 2, select Air Fry, set temperature to 400°F (205°C) and set time to 25 minutes.
5. Stir the potato sticks at least three times during cooking.
6. Meanwhile, make the gravy: Heat the butter in a saucepan over medium heat until melted.
7. Add the onion, thyme, and garlic and sauté for 5 minutes or until the onion is translucent.
8. Add the flour and sauté for an additional 2 minutes. Pour in the tomato paste and beef stock and cook for 1 more minute or until lightly thickened.
9. Drizzle the gravy with Worcestershire sauce and sprinkle with salt and ground black pepper. Reduce the heat to low to keep the gravy warm until ready to serve.
10. When done, the sticks should be golden brown. Remove from the oven. Transfer the fried potato sticks onto a plate, then sprinkle with salt and ground black pepper. Scatter with string cheese and pour the gravy over. Serve warm.

Arancini

Ingredients:

Servings: 10
Cooking Time:
30 Mins.

- » ⅔ C. raw white Arborio rice
- » 2 tsp. butter
- » ½ tsp. salt
- » 1⅓ C. water
- » 2 large eggs, well beaten
- » 1¼ C. seasoned Italian-style dried bread crumbs
- » 10 ¾-inch semi-firm Mozzarella cubes
- » Cooking spray

Directions:

1. Pour the rice, butter, salt, and water in a pot. Stir to mix well and bring a boil over medium-high heat. Keep stirring.
2. Reduce the heat to low and cover the pot. Simmer for 20 minutes or until the rice is tender.
3. Turn off the heat and let sit, covered, for 10 minutes, then open the lid and fluffy the rice with a fork. Allow to cool for 10 more minutes.
4. Pour the beaten eggs in a bowl, then pour the bread crumbs in a separate bowl.
5. Scoop 2 tbsp. of the cooked rice up and form it into a ball, then press the Mozzarella into the ball and wrap.
6. Dredge the ball in the eggs first, then shake the excess off the dunk the ball in the bread crumbs. Roll to coat evenly. Repeat to make 10 balls in total with remaining rice.
7. Transfer the balls in the air fryer basket and spritz with cooking spray.
8. Put the air fryer basket on the baking pan and slide into Rack Position 2, select Air Fry, set temperature to 375°F (190°C) and set time to 10 minutes.
9. When cooking is complete, the balls should be lightly browned and crispy.
10. Remove the balls from the oven and allow to cool before serving.

Chicken Sausage And Broccoli Casserole

Ingredients:

Servings: 8
Cooking Time:
20 Mins.

- » 10 eggs
- » 1 C. Cheddar cheese, shredded and divided
- » ¾ C. heavy whipping cream
- » 1 (12-ounce / 340-g) package cooked chicken sausage
- » 1 C. broccoli, chopped
- » 2 cloves garlic, minced
- » ½ tbsp. salt
- » ¼ tbsp. ground black pepper
- » Cooking spray

Directions:

1. Spritz the baking pan with cooking spray.
2. Whisk the eggs with Cheddar and cream in a large bowl to mix well.
3. Combine the cooked sausage, broccoli, garlic, salt, and ground black pepper in a separate bowl. Stir to mix well.
4. Pour the sausage mixture into the baking pan, then spread the egg mixture over to cover.
5. Slide the baking pan into Rack Position 1, select Convection Bake, set temperature to 400°F (205°C) and set time to 20 minutes.
6. When cooking is complete, the egg should be set and a toothpick inserted in the center should come out clean.
7. Serve immediately.

Classic Churros

Ingredients:

Servings: 12
Cooking Time:
10 Mins.

- » 4 tbsp. butter
- » ¼ tsp. salt
- » ½ C. water
- » ½ C. all-purpose flour
- » 2 large eggs
- » 2 tsp. ground cinnamon
- » ¼ C. granulated white sugar
- » Cooking spray

Directions:

1. Put the butter, salt, and water in a saucepan. Bring to a boil until the butter is melted on high heat. Keep stirring.
2. Reduce the heat to medium and fold in the flour to form a dough. Keep cooking and stirring until the dough is dried out and coat the pan with a crust.
3. Turn off the heat and scrape the dough in a large bowl. Allow to cool for 15 minutes.
4. Break and whisk the eggs into the dough with a hand mixer until the dough is sanity and firm enough to shape.
5. Scoop up 1 tbsp. of the dough and roll it into a ½-inch-diameter and 2-inch-long cylinder. Repeat with remaining dough to make 12 cylinders in total.
6. Combine the cinnamon and sugar in a large bowl and dunk the cylinders into the cinnamon mix to coat.
7. Arrange the cylinders on a plate and refrigerate for 20 minutes.
8. Spritz the air fryer basket with cooking spray. Place the cylinders in the basket and spritz with cooking spray.
9. Put the air fryer basket on the baking pan and slide into Rack Position 2, select Air Fry, set temperature to 375ºF (190ºC) and set time to 10 minutes.
10. Flip the cylinders halfway through the cooking time.
11. When cooked, the cylinders should be golden brown and fluffy.
12. Serve immediately.

Chicken Ham Casserole

Ingredients:

Servings: 4 - 6
Cooking Time:
15 Mins.

» 2 C. diced cooked chicken

» 1 C. diced ham

» ¼ tsp. ground nutmeg

» ½ C. half-and-half

» ½ tsp. ground black pepper

» 6 slices Swiss cheese

» Cooking spray

Directions:

1. Spritz the baking pan with cooking spray.

2. Combine the chicken, ham, nutmeg, half-and-half, and ground black pepper in a large bowl. Stir to mix well.

3. Pour half of the mixture into the baking pan, then top the mixture with 3 slices of Swiss cheese, then pour in the remaining mixture and top with remaining cheese slices.

4. Slide the baking pan into Rack Position 1, select Convection Bake, set temperature to 350ºF (180ºC) and set time to 15 minutes.

5. When cooking is complete, the egg should be set and the cheese should be melted.

6. Serve immediately.

Sumptuous Beef And Bean Chili Casserole

Ingredients:

Servings: 4
Cooking Time: 31 Mins.

» 1 tbsp. olive oil
» ½ C. finely chopped bell pepper
» ½ C. chopped celery
» 1 onion, chopped
» 2 garlic cloves, minced
» 1 lb. (454 g) ground beef
» 1 can diced tomatoes
» ½ tsp. parsley
» ½ tbsp. chili powder
» 1 tsp. chopped cilantro
» 1½ C. vegetable broth
» 1 (8-ounce / 227-g) can cannellini beans
» Salt and ground black pepper, to taste

Directions:

1. Heat the olive oil in a nonstick skillet over medium heat until shimmering.
2. Add the bell pepper, celery, onion, and garlic to the skillet and sauté for 5 minutes or until the onion is translucent.
3. Add the ground beef and sauté for an additional 6 minutes or until lightly browned.
4. Mix in the tomatoes, parsley, chili powder, cilantro and vegetable broth, then cook for 10 more minutes. Stir constantly.
5. Pour them in the baking pan, then mix in the beans and sprinkle with salt and ground black pepper.
6. Slide the baking pan into Rack Position 1, select Convection Bake, set temperature to 350°F (180°C) and set time to 10 minutes.
7. When cooking is complete, the vegetables should be tender and the beef should be well browned.
8. Remove from the oven and serve immediately.

Simple Cheesy Shrimps

Ingredients:

Servings: 4 - 6
Cooking Time:
8 Mins.

» ⅔ C. grated Parmesan cheese

» 4 minced garlic cloves

» 1 tsp. onion powder

» ½ tsp. oregano

» 1 tsp. basil

» 1 tsp. ground black pepper

» 2 tbsp. olive oil

» 2 lb. (907 g) cooked large shrimps, peeled and deveined

» Lemon wedges, for topping

» Cooking spray

Directions:

1. Spritz the air fryer basket with cooking spray.

2. Combine all the ingredients, except for the shrimps, in a large bowl. Stir to mix well.

3. Dunk the shrimps in the mixture and toss to coat well. Shake the excess off. Arrange the shrimps in the basket.

4. Put the air fryer basket on the baking pan and slide into Rack Position 2, select Air Fry, set temperature to 350°F (180°C) and set time to 8 minutes.

5. Flip the shrimps halfway through the cooking time.

6. When cooking is complete, the shrimps should be opaque. Transfer the cooked shrimps onto a large plate and squeeze the lemon wedges over before serving.

Milton Keynes UK
Ingram Content Group UK Ltd.
UKHW050014270124
436745UK00010B/420